MW00831097

LEARNING FROM
THE MASTER
TEACHER

TIMOTHY N. WADE

ISBN 978-1-68526-679-0 (Paperback)
ISBN 978-1-68526-680-6 (Digital)

Copyright © 2023 Timothy N. Wade
All rights reserved
First Edition

All rights reserved. No part of this publication may be reproduced, distributed, or transmitted in any form or by any means, including photocopying, recording, or other electronic or mechanical methods without the prior written permission of the publisher. For permission requests, solicit the publisher via the address below.

Covenant Books
11661 Hwy 707
Murrells Inlet, SC 29576
www.covenantbooks.com

To my parents, Neil and Lela Wade, thank you for always pointing me toward the Master Teacher. I love you!

CONTENTS

INTRODUCTION

Teaching is one of the oldest professions in the world. Every civilization, culture, and society has depended on the work of teachers. Behind every great ruler, statesman, philosopher, tradesman, clergy, and citizen, there was a teacher. Every guild, career, trade, and vocation exist because of the work of an educator. People must learn, and teachers are there to instruct them. Everyone, whether they know it or not, has benefited from the dedication of a teacher.

Jesus was a teacher. He is best known around the world for this role. Yet as this book will reveal, He was more than just a mere teacher. Since He was the embodiment of God in human form, He was the exemplar of teachers—the Master Teacher.

I surmise that if you are reading this book, you are a Christian. As such, it is not difficult for you to make the direct correlation between Christ's perfection as the Son of God and His unblemished role as the Master Teacher. However, if you are not a Christian, I would like to reassure you that this book is for you as well. By studying the role of the Master Teacher, all will benefit from the Nazarene who was the epitome of all the wisdom, knowledge, and love we could ever hope to encounter.

As we allow ourselves to learn from Jesus Christ, we will become better teachers by either laying a foundation for faith or strengthening the one we already have. Either way, as we learn from the Master Teacher, we will be transformed.

CHAPTER 1

DISCOVERING JESUS IN THE CLASSROOM

Humming lights reflected off the white laminate floors. Student-made posters and anti-drug PSAs plastered the brick walls. Trophies and plaques of academic and athletic achievements filled wood-and-glass cases along one wall. The scent of floor wax, old books, crayons, and pencils hung thick in the air.

As I walked down the hallway before my first day as a full-fledged teacher, these sights and smells reminded me of the years I spent within school buildings as a student. Now I was the teacher.

I felt like I belonged here.

After all, I was carrying on a family heritage that had begun with my great-grandfather. He traveled as an itinerate teacher in the Central Texas countryside in the early twentieth century. My father continued the tradition by serving as an educator, as did three of his five children. I thought being a fourth-generation educator would prepare me for my first year of teaching.

I was wrong.

I stood on the starting line of my career, and I was eager to come off the blocks and start my career with grit and determination. Yet like many who enter this field, I could never have predicted the challenges I would have to hurdle in my first year of teaching.

My initial dose of reality came with my first paycheck. The amount was barely above the state base for a new teacher, but I thought I had hit the jackpot after counting loose change to buy gas as a college student. That was September. By October, I winced at how much of my paycheck disappeared after paying for my classroom start-up costs, living expenses, and student loans.

Another unexpected expense drained my wages: food…but not for me. Most of the students at the tiny rural school where I began my career came from impoverished families. Many of the students who entered my class were always hungry. They dragged into my classroom with glazed eyes and listless bodies. For many of my students, the school lunch was often the only decent meal they ate during the day, and that was not saying much. As anyone who has filed through a cafeteria serving line will tell you, the food and proportions often leave much to be desired.

I knew if my famished students were going to function in my classroom, they needed nutritious food. Soon, the two lower drawers of my filing cabinet housed the healthiest snacks I could buy. Throughout the day, any student who needed something to eat could go to the filing cabinet and grab a snack. At first, I was concerned they would swarm the cabinet like a pack of eager wolves, but I was rewarded with very grateful students.

Almost instantly, I noticed a difference in them. Not only were my students able to pay attention but also they genuinely wanted to participate and perform well in class. I believe that this was their way of repaying the favor of my meeting one of their basic needs. As one student who was introduced to me as a key troublemaker remarked a few days after I started supplying food, "If you keep the food coming, I'll keep listening!"

He was true to his word.

After keeping the drawers filled for a few weeks, I was startled to discover the snacks were gobbling my personal finances. After all, it was mainly growing teenage boys for whom I was buying food. I was thankful when the school district hired a paraprofessional, the wife of a local doctor, halfway through the first semester. She took on the financial burden of buying food, and even clothing, for our students in need.

I was humbled to discover the condition of my students. Of course, I had heard about students living in severe poverty. However, seeing it firsthand shook me. I found it hard to relate to their plight since I had never gone to school hungry. I did not know what it was like to be so famished that I could not function in a classroom.

The initial confidence I felt during my first few days as a teacher evaporated after I saw the state of my students. Their needs forced me to reevaluate what it meant to be a teacher. My students needed food, and I wanted to give them what they needed. Once my students' basic needs were met, they did more than learn—they thrived.

The Desire to Provide

This experience made a deep impact on me, especially on my spiritual life. I was burdened to pray for my students and their situations, and that burden pushed me to read the Bible, especially the gospels, in a different light. The accounts of Jesus teaching people struck me in a new way. Up to this point, I had never really thought of the Lord as an educator. In my mind, He was always someone altogether separate from my experience. I knew it was proper to revere Him as the Son of God, and therefore, He was perfect in all He did. If He taught, He did so flawlessly. How could I relate to Him?

Thankfully, after reflecting on the story of Jesus providing food for the hungry crowd of five thousand people—His students—I was both humbled and encouraged. He recognized the spiritual and physical needs of His students and made sure their basic need for food was met to assure their spiritual need for truth was uninhibited.

The gospel of John offers a valuable perspective on this story. Fully aware that the disciples did not have enough food to feed the gathering of five thousand people, Jesus commanded His followers to serve dinner to the crowd. John relates an insight into why Jesus made a seemingly impossible command. "He said this to test [His disciples], for He Himself knew what He would do" (John 6:6).

Isn't that just like a teacher?

Jesus seized a teachable moment to invite His followers to learn from Him. With a boy's lunch of bread and fish in hand, Jesus wanted all who gathered to hear Him and, those who would later hear of this account, to pause in preparation to learn.

What was the intended lesson?

He wanted His students to see that He was the absolute provider of all good things. He was the One who created humans with the need to consume food. He was also the One who provided the food for humans to eat. Through the miraculous act of multiplying a humble meal to feed a multitude, Jesus taught He could fulfill all needs. This principle is affirmed in the fact that He did not simply furnish the means for the food to be acquired; He created the food itself. Once He provided for the need, He then allowed His disciples to participate in His work—a key point we will revisit later.

In providing food, Jesus displayed His love for those who learned from Him. Through this miracle, Jesus demonstrated that the true heart of a teacher is essentially a servant dedicated to the enlightenment and betterment of others. Jesus did not simply want His followers to learn; He wanted them fulfilled.

Most people acknowledge that an educator's role is to impart knowledge and understanding to learners. However, any astute teacher quickly realizes so much more is involved in this process. A teacher desires to meet the needs of their students' hearts and minds. Whether the students' needs are academic, guidance in making decisions, or as fundamental as physical nourishment and clothing, teachers desire that their students have everything they require to add to their knowledge, which will lead them to fulfilling their God-given purpose. This desire was at the heart of Jesus's entire teaching ministry.

We have the opportunity to follow Christ's example and honor Him as we serve our students. When faced with the needs for those in my classroom, I recognized my opportunity to imitate Jesus—the Master Teacher. I often failed. Yet even in my failures, I was thankful because I discovered the honor to be more than a mere transmitter of knowledge. I had the sacred job of imitating the One who is the *way*, the *truth*, and the *life* (see John 14:6).

By the end of my first year, I knew I was officially present at the school as a teacher, but I had a more important job of being an example of Christ to my students. I could not speak openly about my faith, but I could represent the Master Teacher by example. If I could not use my words, then my actions had to resound clearly.

An Act of Worship through Imitation

As we imitate Christ as the Master Teacher, we discover that the task of educating our students emerges as an act of worship. Jesus invites us, just as He did His disciples, to participate in His work of proclaiming His truth. As we labor to inform others about the truth of Christ, we are worshipping Him in spirit and in truth (see John 4:24). Some of us teach in public schools or other institutions that prohibit us from speaking openly about our relationship with Christ. Yet the truth of Jesus Christ can be found whenever and wherever an honest perspective of the world and humanity are taught.

Christ is the creator and sustainer of all existence. As such, we encounter Him in every subject area we teach. In mathematics, we see His logic, immutability, and orderliness. In the sciences, we deduce His genius in the harmony, orderliness, and purpose of the universe He created. Even within language arts and literature, we experience His expressiveness in revealing Himself as the Logos—the living Word of God (see John 1). The authentic nature of academia, from the stalwart laws of nature to the loftiest concepts of philosophy, declares the person of Jesus Christ. As we teach truth, we reveal Jesus is the way, the truth, and the life who allows all humanity to learn how He created and sustains the world.

Chances are that if you are reading this book, you are a teacher. Whether that means you teach at a public or private school, at a parochial or church institution, or in the homeschool setting, you have the opportunity to worship and honor the Master Teacher as you imitate Him.

Of course, all Christians should keep this mentality at the forefront of their minds. As the Apostle Paul underscored, "Therefore, we are ambassadors for Christ, as though God were making an appeal through us" (2 Corinthians 5:20 NASB). However, teachers are in a unique position to make an appeal through their skills.

Many will assume that being an educator who strives to imitate Christ, as the Master Teacher, begins and ends at simply being a Christian who happens to have a job as a teacher. In broad terms, this is true. However, I would suggest that a Christian educator can never reach his or her fullest potential without purposefully investigating and imitating the role of Jesus as *the* Master Teacher.

The Bible has revealed Jesus Christ as the King of kings and Lord of lords. To this grand litany, I would humbly add Teacher of teachers. He is the Master Teacher. It is only when we approach Him, who is the Lord of all truth and Savior of our souls, with the willing heart of a student who desires to be like the Master Teacher, that we ourselves become teachers worthy of that calling.

There are those to whom teaching is just a livelihood. They view their job as a teacher to be just that—a job, merely, a vocation. When all who teach realize that their passion for education and their dedication to Christ can converge within their classroom, like the confluence of two mighty rivers, they will never see what they do as a mere vocation. They will sail through their career with the joy of imitating Jesus and serving their students for His glory.

Chapter 1 discussion questions are the following:
1. When did you know you wanted to be a teacher? What inspired you to teach?
2. How have you tried to honor Jesus as you serve as a teacher?
3. How have you discovered/experienced Christ in the classroom?
4. How can you worship Jesus in your role as a teacher?

CHAPTER 2

JESUS, THE MASTER TEACHER

The description of the online video piqued my interest, so I clicked the link. A man with the microphone stood on a busy sidewalk and asked one simple question: "Who was Jesus Christ?" The camera captured the responses of the people who passed by. Most of their answers were predictable. Some people gave an overview of the life of Jesus and still others acknowledged their faith in Christ. When pressed, a few responders compared Him to other religious figures such as Confucius, Buddha, and Mohammad.

From the variety of responses given, one characteristic echoed in almost every response: the acknowledgment that Jesus was a teacher. Some qualified this statement by describing Him as a "good" or "moral" teacher, but the overwhelming consensus of all those questioned was that Jesus is most widely considered to be a teacher.

Who Is Jesus?

This question is simple to ask, but yet it is powerful enough to echo for centuries. Everyone who has read the teachings of Jesus Christ has wrestled with this question. This inquiry has spurred endless debates, filled countless books, and has, quite frankly, divided the world. According to the Bible, it is a question that no one can escape answering. The Scriptures uncompromisingly decree that how a person responds to it has everlasting consequences.

Major world religions have tried to identify Jesus Christ. Hinduism, Islam, Buddhism, and Judaism all acknowledge that Jesus was, in the very least, a teacher but not the Son of God as Christians recognize Him. Outside the sphere of religion, many philosophers have recognized Jesus as a provocative figure. Some even regarded Him as offering the best answers of life's greatest questions. For example, the seventeenth-century philosopher Baruch Spinoza did not recognize Jesus as anything more than a mere man, but he claimed, "The eternal wisdom of God...has shown itself forth in all things, but chiefly in the mind of man, and most of all in Jesus Christ."[1] It is clear that Jesus is widely considered by many non-Christians a superb communicator of truth and wisdom, in other words, a master teacher.

The views of these prominent thinkers and religions are a starting place for people to understand a key doctrine held by the Christian church. Throughout two thousand years, major figures in the church have regarded Jesus as the exemplar of teachers. Late in the first century, the church father Ignatius declared that Jesus was the "one Teacher, who spoke and it was done."[2] About a century later, Clement of Alexandria recorded a prayer of thanksgiving in which he praised the "Father and Son, Son and Father, the Son, Instructor and Teacher."[3] Martin Luther, the German monk who played a lead role in igniting the Protestant Reformation, declared to his students, "We are to hear Christ, who has been appointed by the Father as our divine Teacher."[4] Another major Reformation leader, John Calvin, acknowledged, "The Apostles had been duly and amply instructed by the best of teachers."[5]

Until the mid-twentieth century, most Christian and secular leaders in education regarded Jesus as the pinnacle of pedagogy. In his volume *History of Education*, secular scholar E. L. Kemp surveyed the role of Jesus as teacher:

> Measured by the nature of the lessons he taught,
> by his method of presenting them, by the num-

ber of persons whom they reached, and by the results they have accomplished, he was the greatest teacher of all teachers.[6]

What influenced such an overwhelming consensus from both Christians and secular people over the centuries? As Roy B. Zuck points out in his wonderful book *Teaching as Jesus Taught*, they were "enthralled with Jesus' superior command of the art of teaching."[7] It is impossible to encounter the life and teachings of Jesus Christ without seeing His supremacy as a teacher.

Why was Jesus the greatest teacher? There are many characteristics Jesus showed as a teacher that we could investigate to determine what made Him the greatest teacher. In fact, many of these key attributes such as loving other people, proclaiming truth, maintaining relationships, and being an effective communicator are discussed in this book. However, it is not a matter of Christ possessing more of these qualities than anyone else that makes Him the greatest teacher. It was the reason why He possessed them (and many others). Jesus was the greatest of all teachers—He is the Master Teacher—because He is God.

Sadly, many people today are ignorant of His role as both. Barna Group published findings that suggest a majority of Americans (92 percent) believe that Jesus was a real, historical person.[8] This majority also acknowledges that Jesus was a spiritual leader and great teacher. However, the percentage of Americans who believe in the deity of Christ plummets among the younger generation (48 percent), indicating a major shift in thinking. Increasingly, people consider Jesus to be a great spiritual leader and teacher who made an unequaled impact upon the world, but they do not accept Him as God incarnate in human form. This stance is a contradiction.

If you believe that Jesus was a great teacher of morals and ethics, someone who proclaimed truth and love, you cannot ignore His claims to be God (see John 1:1, 14–18, 5:18, 10:30–33, 17:21). A truly good and moral teacher does not claim to be God unless he is God. C. S. Lewis offers the best response to this point:

> A man who was merely a man and said the sort of things Jesus said would not be a great moral teacher. He would either be a lunatic on a level with the man who says he is a poached egg or else he would be the Devil of Hell. You must make your choice. Either this man was, and is, the Son of God; or else a madman or something worse. You can shut Him up for a fool, you can spit at Him and kill him as a demon; or you can fall at His feet and call Him Lord and God. But let us not come with any patronizing nonsense about His being a great human teacher. He has not left that open to us. He did not intend to.[9]

Lewis deftly destroys any notion that Jesus was only a product of human imagination or heredity. Nothing in all of fallen humanity could have brought forth such a person on its own. Jesus was truly good; therefore, He was divine and not just a "great human teacher."

When we refer to Jesus as the "Master Teacher" and explore the qualities and actions He exhibited, we are not saying that He was the best example humanity could produce from itself. Although He was, and is, the example all Christians should aspire to be like, His origins are beyond the human realm. He is the Master Teacher because in Him is the fullness of God.

Philosopher and theologian Thomas B. Warren declared:

> Jesus was the incomparable teacher. This fact is compelling evidence in favor of the conclusion that He is the Son of the only true God. He was so marvelously unique as a teacher that He simply could not have been merely a human being. We are driven to the conclusion that He was Divine.[10]

As the full expression of both God and humanity, perhaps one of the most shocking aspects of Jesus's role as the Master Teacher is that He exhibited His work on earth. He revealed Himself at a specific point in history, in a specific geographic location, and within a particular educational system. The holy Creator and Sustainer of all creation stepped down into these particular limitations to become an earthly teacher whom people could see, hear, and touch.

The prophet Isaiah made it clear that nothing about Jesus's physical appearance or social standing signaled that He was God. He did not walk around with a halo crowning is head. "He had no form or majesty that we should look at Him, and no beauty that we should desire Him" (Isaiah 53:2b). The originator of all truth and beauty took on an ordinary form. Likewise, He served in a role that was familiar to people of His day. Yet as we will discover, He was like nothing the world had ever witnessed before or since.

The Role of a Teacher in Christ's Day

The Jewish society of first-century Israel had a well-established and proud educational heritage. Jesus followed many of the norms and conventions of a teacher of His time. To appreciate the example of His style of teaching, we must understand the social and educational constructs in which Jesus taught.

Jesus was a rabbi, a Jewish teacher. The gospels capture this public perception of Christ during His ministry. Whenever one of Jesus's followers addressed Him, they most often referred to Him as either a "rabbi" (Hebrew) or a "didaskalos" (Greek). Both essentially meant "teacher." It is helpful to consider this title against the backdrop of all the other identifiers for Jesus. Throughout the New Testament, Jesus had forty-two various names and titles. Based on the frequency of use, the title of "teacher" ranked fourth after "Jesus," "Lord," and "Son of Man."[11] It is fascinating to note that after the nominal address, the next three names and titles offer a perspective of the Master Teacher's key roles as (1) the Lord of all, (2) the One sent from God to humankind, and (3) a teacher.

The Apostle John does us a great service when, writing to his immediate bilingual readers, he used the two words for "teacher," rabbi and didaskalos, in the following verse:

> When Jesus turned and noticed them following him, he asked them, "What are you looking for?" "They said to him, 'Rabbi (which means "teacher" [*didaskalos*]), where are you staying?'"
> (John 1:38 CSB)

Both terms, in the Hebrew and the Greek, acknowledged a master teacher at the pinnacle of his expertise. In fact, the term *rabbi* was a variation from the Hebrew word for someone who was great or mighty.[12] Twice in the gospels, people called Jesus *rabboni*—a personalized form of rabbi meaning "my teacher" or even "my master." Usage of these titles was nothing new in the first century, but they serve to authenticate the perception of Christ as a respected teacher in His own time.[13]

Like other rabbis, Jesus held the Torah in high regard. What we now refer to as the Old Testament was the only Scripture that existed early in the first century. The hallmark of every rabbi was his dedication to the Old Testament Scriptures or Torah. Originally, the Torah referred to the first five books of the Old Testament (Genesis, Exodus, Leviticus, Numbers, and Deuteronomy). However, by the time of Christ, the term came to encompass all of the Old Testament with an understood division into two main parts: the Law and the prophets.[14]

Rabbis derived numerous teachings and additional commands based on the Torah, but Christ summed up the whole of the Torah in two basic commands: (1) love God with all your heart, soul, and mind; and (2) love others as you love yourself (see Matthew 22:34–40). In this simple, two-part command, the Master Teacher shines as an educator like none other. Instead of compounding the Scriptures, He explains them in a manner that was easy to understand and apply in the lives of His hearers. Christ's distaste of other teachers and "experts of the Law" who added to the Torah was evident when He offered the scathing rebuke: "And you experts in the law, woe to you, because you load people down with burdens they can hardly carry, and you yourselves will not lift one finger to help them" (Luke 11:46 NIV). It is no wonder that many scribes and Pharisees opposed Jesus and His teachings.

Jesus taught in the same way many first-century rabbis applied their trade. At the time of Christ, Israel teemed with itinerate teachers who traveled among the villages, towns, major cities, and even remote areas. They taught in synagogues, open spaces, and even private homes. The gospels record the Lord teaching in all these places.

If you were to witness from a distance a first-century rabbi teaching, you would easily recognize him. As he instructed, he sat while his listeners gathered around him, some sitting at his feet (see Matthew 5:1–2, 26:55; Luke 5:3; 4:20–21). This educational setting seems odd to many modern people who have attended classes where the students sit and the teacher stands. However, as today, the postures of the teacher and learners were meaningful to the educational traditions.

Rabbis amassed students, or disciples, to himself and invited them to emulate his lifestyle and follow his teachings. If a rabbi believed a hearer worthy to be one of his students, he invited that student to follow him. Jesus extended this identical invitation to His disciples (see Matthew 4:19, 8:22, 9:9, 10:38, 16:24; Mark 2:14, 10:21; Luke 5:27, 9:59; John 1:43, 21:19–22).

Disciples were not passive listeners to the teaching of their rabbi. They were dedicated adherents. Although the manner in which Jesus called His disciples was similar to other rabbis, He promised His disciples something greater than any other rabbi could:

> If anyone would come after me, let him deny himself and take up his cross and follow me. For whoever would save his life will lose it, but whoever loses his life for my sake will find it. For what will it profit a man if he gains the whole world and forfeits his soul? Or what shall a man give in return for his soul? (Matthew 16:24–26)

The call of Jesus to His disciples was not unique in the act of the rabbi's offer and the students' expectations; it was radical in the promises made by Christ to His disciples. Christ's disciples would experience more than enlightenment; they would be transformed from ordinary fishermen and tax collectors to those who would change the world with the message of the Master Teacher.

Jesus's disciples came to realize they were not serving a typical rabbi but rather the long-promised Messiah of Israel. In the Gospel of John, we witness many students and followers of Christ leave Him after He identified Himself as the One sent by God to offer eternal life. Those offended declared that His teachings were too difficult to follow. John tells us what happened next:

> After this many of his disciples turned back and no longer walked with him. So Jesus said to the Twelve, "Do you want to go away as well?" Simon Peter answered him, "Lord, to whom shall we go? You have the words of eternal life, and we have believed, and have come to know, that you are the Holy One of God." (John 6:66–69)

The disciples knew they were not following just any rabbi but *the* rabbi—the true Master Teacher. They did not always understand the things He taught or foretold, but much of it became clearer after Jesus's resurrection. Before Pentecost and the coming of the Holy Spirit, the disciples were as impulsive, self-interested, hardheaded, and ignorant as we all are without God's grace. Even so, the things Jesus taught were so extraordinary and His work so powerful; the apostles realized that Jesus alone had "the words of eternal life," and they followed Him even when others turned away.

Jesus wants to teach us. As Christian teachers, our Master Teacher has called us, like He did His disciples, to follow Him.

Following the Master Teacher

As first-century rabbis traveled to spread their teachings in an age before mass communication, they walked the dusty roads and paths of Israel. The rabbi led His entourage of learners, teaching along the way as He kicked up dust with every step. This visual of the dusty, road-weary scholar sitting as He instructed His disciples was a common, even venerated, image at the time of Christ. The Mishnah, a collection of rabbinic teachings from around the time of Christ, offers an exhortation of this practice:

> May your house be a meeting house for Sages,
> become dirty in the dust of their feet and drink
> their words thirstily.[15]

The term used for *sages* (*hakam*) is best translated as "a skilled or wise person," but it was understood to be synonymous with a rabbi. This word picture is powerful, displaying that just as the dust that fell from the rabbi should stick to his disciples, so should his teachings adhere to them as they eagerly take in his words. To follow a rabbi was to allow his teaching and way of life to cover you.

This imagery reminds me of where I grew up in Central Texas. Many of the roads I traveled were dirt roads of caliche. This mineral works well as a paving material, but during the dry summers, it becomes a cloud of fine dust that billows behind moving vehicles like smoke from a rocket. A thick film of caliche dust covered everything bordering the roads—trees, buildings, fence lines, even livestock. It was easy to recognize the cars and trucks that traveled these roads by their chalky dusty-brown discoloration.

There is no doubt that Peter, James, John, and the other disciples were proud to wear the dust of their rabbi. Keeping in mind that to be a Christian means to be a disciple of Jesus Christ; obvious questions arise: Are we following our Master Teacher faithfully? Are people able to recognize the One we follow by the "dust" on us? Do we thirst for His words and listen to them attentively? Do we teach others how they can also follow the Master Teacher?

Disciples to Teachers

All Christians are called, like the first disciples of Christ, to follow our Master Rabbi. We are to emulate Him and represent Him well in our complete dedication to Him. Christian educators are obligated to make sure we know the teaching of our rabbi and to follow His example faithfully. In doing so, we are not only good disciples but also great teachers.

This transformation begins when we realize that we are disciples-teachers. Note the order of this title; it is important. We are foremost students covered in the dust of our Master Teacher striving to be like Him. Even so, we are disciples who have a mission: to teach the truth of God as revealed in the Bible and attest to it by our own life experiences. Our continual process of learning from Jesus while teaching others about Him never ends.

This process walks alongside what teachers have always known: we are lifelong learners. Over the past few decades, secular education has discovered the importance of promoting lifelong learning for teachers. The premise of this advice is that when a teacher is engaged in the learning process for themselves, they perform better as teachers while instilling a dedication to lifelong learning in their students. The evidence-based research for this claim is growing. As educational researcher Christopher Day remarked: "One of the main tasks of all teachers is to inculcate in their students a disposition toward lifelong learning. They must, therefore, demonstrate their own commitment towards and enthusiasm for lifelong learning."[16]

In response, many state educational agencies and school accreditation organizations encourage lifelong learning by requiring teachers to take classes to keep their teaching skills sharp. These agencies place such an emphasis on this concept that teachers who do not fulfill their required training face suspension of their teaching credentials.

Before all the contemporary scholarly evidence and requirements for lifelong learning existed, the Bible commanded followers of God always to pursue learning. Wisdom, instruction, understanding, and knowledge are interchangeable synonyms within the biblical framework that refers to what we would collectively call "learning." The book of Proverbs offers perfect examples of the interconnected use of these terms.

> My son, if you receive my words and treasure up my commandments with you, making your ear attentive to wisdom and inclining your heart to understanding; yes, if you call out for insight and raise your voice for understanding, if you seek it like silver and search for it as for hidden treasures, then you will understand the fear of the LORD and find the knowledge of God. For the LORD gives wisdom; from His mouth come knowledge and understanding. (Proverbs 2:1–6)

King Solomon wrote most of the book of Proverbs, including the passage above. God gave him the opportunity to ask for anything he desired. What did King Solomon want most? Wisdom—he desired to learn. He understood that all the riches and power in this life could not compare with understanding the truth of God, the world, and his place in it. God honored Solomon's request and gave him more wisdom and understanding than any other human possessed (see 1 Kings 3:5–14). If King Solomon, also known as "The Teacher," pleased God by pursuing learning; we should do likewise (see Ecclesiastes 1).

As Christian educators, what is our ultimate goal as lifelong learners? The goal is not to learn but to be more like the Master Teacher. Once again, this is the aim for every Christian, but for the Christian educator, this is the process of examining the work and life of Jesus Christ as He was originally regarded a teacher.

In the following chapters, we will discover the work of Christ as a teacher and thereby gain a clearer picture of how we can learn from the Master Teacher.

Chapter 2 discussion questions are the following:
1. How have you heard other people describe Jesus?

2. How would others describe your relationship with the Master Teacher?
3. If your students who do not know Jesus were to describe the Master Teacher based on your example, what would they say?
4. How are you, as a disciple of Jesus, pursuing your role as a lifelong learner?

CHAPTER 3

TRUTH

"What is truth?"

The question echoed off the walls of the Roman judgment hall. The Roman government official Pontus Pilate asked the question as he looked upon the battered and bloodied Jewish teacher standing before him. Outside, a crowd shouted for the young teacher's death. Pilate asked this simple, but profound, question more from desperation than honest inquiry.

Moments before asking the question, Pilate interrogated Jesus hoping to find a way in which to save the young rabbi from the crowd's bloodlust. During this inquiry, Jesus summarized His life's mission: "For this I have been born, and for this I have come into the world, to testify to the truth. Everyone who is of the truth hears My voice." To this declaration, a dispirited Pilate could only retort, "What is truth?" (John 18:37–38 NASB)

Pilate's inquiry is, perhaps, the oldest and most fundamental question posed by every human mind. Although some people may not state it as succinctly as Pilate, everyone has asked a form of this question at some point in life. Some ask it internally, almost imperceptibly, as they try to figure out the world and their purpose in it. Others who dare voice their inquiry have made it an essential philosophical query. Whichever way it is asked, the fundamental question has reverberated throughout human history. Even within our post-

19

modern culture that tries to strip the objective and absolute nature from truth, people still wonder: "What is truth?"

What Is Truth?

Jesus communicated truth in everything He said and did. There was never a moment when He spoke or acted falsely. One of His closest disciples, Peter, testified to the integrity of his teacher by acknowledging that Jesus "committed no sin, neither was deceit found in his mouth" (1 Peter 2:22). If anyone would have witnessed a falsehood committed by Jesus, either purposefully or accidentally, it would have been this disciple. Why did Peter stress this point? Was it to identify Jesus as merely a good, moral teacher? No. Peter described his Master Teacher as being the perfect proclaimer and representative of truth.

Jesus spoke clearly on this subject. He identified Himself as being "the way, the *truth*, and the life" (John 14:6, emphasis mine). This self-identification by Jesus revealed that He was not only a practitioner of the truth; He was the truth. This identity made Him unique as a teacher because He was the very substance of what He taught. No mere human teacher can do this. We might instruct others on matters that are common to all people. However, these shared experiences do not originate from a single person. We may even lecture on our own personal experiences; still, we are relating only our interactions with the wider reality of the world. Because the Master Teacher is the God who establishes objective truth by His very existence, He could never have been or ever be anything but truthful. In Him, we learn from the source of truth, not because He described this virtue best, but because He is its originator.

Think of it this way. We depend on light to illuminate the world around us in order for us to understand how it works. It is a major medium used to explore and comprehend the reality of our universe. We use the entire light spectrum, from the visible to the invisible, to expose this reality. What if light itself were a person that was capable and willing to communicate its essence to us? What insights would we learn? Granted, this analogy only goes so far, but it is the manner in which the Bible invites us to think of Jesus Christ (see John 8:12). He is the light of the world who vanquishes darkness, sparks a beacon for the lost, and shines forth truth to all who seek Him. He is the fullness of God's truth, and when He taught, truth illuminated truth.

The Bible reveals that truth is all the principles and concepts derived from God and displayed in Jesus Christ (see 1 John 5:20). Pastor John MacArthur describes truth as "that which is consistent with the mind, will, character, glory, and being of God. Even more to the point: Truth is the self-expression of God."[17]

As the self-expression of God, Jesus revealed that He is the creator of all things, their constant sustainer, and the redeemer of all who place their faith in Him. Anything that harmonizes with this revelation is truth. Conversely, anything that denies or opposes this revelation is error or the opposite of truth.

Everything in creation, by its very existence or by its volition, either confirms or denies truth. Inanimate and nonliving objects display truth as they showcase the artistry of the Creator. To this end, laced throughout the Bible are descriptions of how creation exists as a monument to God's steadfastness and creative genius. The Psalmist proclaimed, "The heavens declare the glory of God, and the sky above proclaims His handiwork. Day to day pours out speech, and night to night reveals knowledge. There is no speech, nor are there words, whose voice is not heard" (Psalm 19:1).

The Apostle Paul added to this theme to underscore that God created the universe to reveal His true nature to all humanity: "For His invisible attributes, namely, His eternal power and divine nature, have been clearly perceived, ever since the creation of the world, in the things that have been made. So they are without excuse" (Romans 1:20).

God created all of us with free will, curiosity, the capacity to learn, and the opportunity to perceive and learn about our universe. We use these to either submit or oppose the truth of our Creator. Scripture indicates we are placed within a creation that proclaims the truth of God for the sole purpose to know Him, to understand the truth that emanates from Him, and to use that truth to honor

Him. The fundamental task of a teacher is to help others find the full measure of this truth.

What I have described so far is called "general revelation" or "natural revelation." General revelation is the theological tenet that maintains that God has established creation as a means to reveal the truth of His character and personality. Therefore, God has given humans the rational capacity and senses to examine and interact within the world to discover truth. Everything that is explored, investigated, and verified points back to the personal Creator who desires to be known.

If you were to ask people how they could be sure that something could be declared as true, most people would make an appeal to science. They would rest on the assumption that the scientific method is the best approach to gain a firm footing on how to classify something as "true."

Indeed, scientific observation is a wonderful approach which utilizes human senses, logic, and reasoning to determine what is factual and probable and subsequently strives to dismiss anything in error or impossible. Traditional Christian doctrine extols this approach. In fact, it should come as no surprise that modern scientific reasoning was founded upon biblical truths. In his investigation of the growth of the modern scientific perspective, Dr. Francis A. Schaeffer explains, "The rise of modern science did not conflict with what the Bible teaches; indeed, at a crucial point the Scientific Revolution rested upon what the Bible teaches...modern science was born out of the Christian world view."[18]

Whether or not they know it or wish to acknowledge it, all scientists, mathematicians, philosophers, artists, and educators are concerned with exploring, chronicling, and teaching God's natural revelation.

Christian teachers have an enriched perspective of natural revelation and how it relates to truth. We understand that the core impetus of our task is to make the fullness of truth known to our students. In short, we are tasked with making Jesus Christ known, but we must begin with the world around us. We must begin with describing how a personal, rational God created the universe. From this vantage point, we can point out how the fingerprints of the Creator are everywhere from the subatomic particles to the expanse of galaxies.

Along with the whole macrocosm bearing witness to the existence of God, we also have access to an understanding that transcends natural revelation: the special revelation of Jesus Christ. As we have already explored, truth is the self-expression of God. In Jesus, we see this self-expression as a man. One of the Master Teacher's disciples, John, explained how Jesus was the very truth of God, or "logos." *Logos* is a Greek word that translates as "word" and embodies the concept of the "Word of God."[19] For our purposes, we denote this "logos" or "word" as truth.

> In the beginning was the Word, and the Word was with God, and the Word was God. He was in the beginning with God. All things came into being through Him, and apart from Him nothing came into being that has come into being. In Him was life, and the life was the Light of men. The Light shines in the darkness, and the darkness did not comprehend it…And the Word became flesh, and dwelt among us, and we saw His glory, glory as of the only begotten from the Father, full of grace and truth. (John 1:1–5, 14 NASB)

Jesus, the Word of truth, who created our universe, became a human so we could learn from Him and comprehend what it cost Him to redeem us and the entire created order. Jesus became one of us so He could be our Master Teacher to the glory of God the Father.

The Attack on Truth

A war is raging in our culture against the truth of God. The attack is on multiple fronts. These corrosive barrages on God's truth are evident in many areas of society: from family and marriage to governance and economics and in every level of education. The attack is widespread, but it is also strategic. Every societal sector is dependent upon the others like arches of a bridge. If one cannot bear the weight, it destroys the function of the whole structure.

One example that underscores this point is the pernicious attacks on the family. This is a strategic assault since the family unit is the basic element of any society. If compromised, all other areas of society, including education, eventually crumble. Dr. James Dobson expresses his thoughts on this matter:

> It is my view that our society can be no more stable than the foundation of individual family units upon which it rests. Our government, our institutions, our schools...indeed, our way of life are dependent on healthy marriages and loyalty to the vulnerable little children around our feet.

The past few decades have witnessed the acceleration of family decay. Families have been ruined by divorce, gutted by parents who lack the courage to discipline their children, and decomposed by the allowance and normalization of every kind of sexual perversion. The enemy's aim is calculated to cleave the feet out from under human society its most vital support: the family.

This attack that started on the family has sent educational institutions reeling. Many universities, colleges, secondary and elementary schools have kowtowed to the demands of a falling society in which truth is relative and rotting perversions are propped up like a corpse to be accepted and celebrated. Many educational institutions who once had have proud heritages of defenders of truth are now, like many of their students, disintegrating the further they go from the truth of God. They produce students who are unable to withstand the challenges that life will hurl at them.

Research strongly suggests that students do better in traditional families, especially in the area of educational attainment.[20] Consider your own experiences. How well do students from crumbling families perform in your class? Of course, there are always exceptions, but dysfunctional families usually hinder students academically. With this in view, it is evident that a crucial battle is being waged in the area of education.

Like any deft general anticipating the enemy's battle strategy, it is important for us to understand the attack on truth. Thankfully, the Apostle Paul witnessed this attack two thousand years ago and offered the readers of his many letters countermeasures to this assault.

Continuing the passage from the first chapter of Romans we referenced earlier, Paul describes how some people will see the evidence of God's truth presented in creation, yet they choose to ignore it.

> For even though they knew God, they did not honor Him as God or give thanks, but they became futile in their speculations, and their foolish heart was darkened. Professing to be wise, they became fools, and exchanged the glory of the incorruptible God for an image in the form of corruptible man and of birds and four-footed animals and crawling creatures. Therefore God gave them over in the lusts of their hearts to impurity, so that their bodies would be dishonored among them. For they exchanged the truth of God for a lie, and worshiped and served the creature rather than the Creator, who is blessed forever. Amen. (Romans 1:21–25 NASB)

The Apostle Paul also warned his protégé, Timothy, of this attack:

> For the time will come when they will not endure sound doctrine; but *wanting* to have their ears tickled, they will accumulate for themselves teachers in accordance to their own desires, and will turn away their ears from the truth and will turn aside to myths. (2 Timothy 4:3–4 NASB)

Paul described with clarity the central attack on truth. The truth of God is displayed for all to see, but many choose either to ignore or oppose it. Willful ignorance and defiance are attacks on truth since both deny the nature and character of God displayed in His creation.

Nonetheless, this denial of truth is not due only to human sin. Satan, the enemy of God, has established a world system that opposes truth by blinding many people to the obvious displays of God's presence and work all around them. As we have already seen, governments, cultures, academia, and the arts are all susceptible to the infection of this system that the New Testament refers to simply as "the world." These areas of civilization that could honor God by proclaiming His truth are attacked, distorted, and used to deny God's truth.

Nowhere is this infection more obvious than in education. Entrenched within every level of modern academia is opposition to objective truth. The abandonment of the foundation of absolute truth ushered in the belief in a subjective, relativistic version of so-called "truth." Society has suffered from this exchange.

Education founded upon God's truth is vital to the health of a society. It offers a pathology to determine what parts of society are diseased with the denial of truth and offers remedies to cut them out like a cancerous tumor. Like any aggressive form of cancer, if it is left untreated, it will spread to other areas. If the institutions charged to educate children are sick, the natural consequences will be a decline in the health of a society and the viral infection of a nation's culture. On the other hand, when education focuses on acknowledging and transmitting truth, a civilization will flourish like a tree planted by a stream (see Psalm 1:3).

Prolific historian Will Durant summed up the effects of this deterioration: "A great civilization is not conquered from without until it has destroyed itself within."[21] Nothing destroys a civilization faster than its departure from an absolute standard of truth. Regrettably, this is the condition of most of the societies and cultures in the world. Secular humanism replaced absolute truth within these societies by first ignoring the Creator and extolling creation in His place. They trade the self-expressive truth of God for the lie (see

Romans 1). What is this lie? It is the same poisonous deception that was first spewed in the garden of Eden. It is the myth that we do not need God: that we are all we need. This lethal lie completely wrecked humanity with its potency, and its effects are clearly seen throughout history up to today.

All this sounds bleak, but as we all know, it is a correct description of our modern world. A clear demonstration of this corruption can be seen during a quick scan through social media on any given day. Trending topics of hatred, greed, pridefulness, and anger are easy to find. Social media is a neutral medium that can be used for all kinds of wonderful uses. Sadly, it often serves as a magnifying glass that amplifies the worse flaws of many people who post things they would never say in person. In many ways, it is an ever-present reminder of the world reeling like a diseased and dying person. There is hope. There is hope because of the Master Teacher.

Defending Truth

Truth can never be defeated because God cannot be overthrown. Although the world system and many people within it trade the truth of God for the lie, God's truth remains unshakable. The world hobbles along under the scars of denial, but the good news is that God offers a cure. Just as a disease can be cured and a broken bone reset, so the foundation of absolute truth can be rebuilt in the lives of people. The cure begins with faith in the Master Teacher.

This good news, or gospel, is the central message of Christianity. As we will examine further in chapter 12, Jesus commissioned His disciples to teach truth and share His gospel. This commission is now in the hands of Christian teachers who are on the front lines defending society from spiraling into the ignorance of moral ambiguity and lies. We are defenders of truth. We are the last voice for absolute truth in the educational sphere which is infected with the anti-truth worldview.

We are tasked with presenting a strong and clear response to the decline we see all around us. Yet we are assured that this battle is nothing new (see 2 Timothy 3:13). The process of people turning from truth and embracing falsehoods is a common theme in human history. The reason is simple: human history is the story of sinful humanity who, left to our own devices, is destined to spiral into deterioration and decay. But the one thing that will preserve society is the adherence to the truth established by God.

We cannot be passive defenders of the truth. On the contrary, we must be aware of the sickness of relativism all around us and work to eradicate it. Truth is truth for all times, all people, and all circumstances. The nature of truth does not change because it is founded in God. So this battle is far more than the clash of two opinions or even two worldviews. It comes down to a matter of life and death, or more specifically, it is a matter of eternal life and eternal death.

I present the defense of truth in such resolute terms because it is a dire matter. Discovering the Master Teacher as the Truth, surrendering to His lordship, and obeying His teachings is the only way a person can find the life God desires them to have, both in this life and the eternal state to come.

Let me offer you a situation that underscores the critical need for someone to follow the Master Teacher. Let's say the only cure for a particular disease is a single medical treatment. Other treatments have been tried, but they only deal with the symptoms of the disease and not its cause. Lives have been saved because of this treatment, and lives have been lost without it. Years of research has proven that this single treatment results in full recovery from the disease in 100 percent of the cases. Let's again say that your doctor has diagnosed you with this disease. His prognosis is that you will experience thorough healing through this therapy. Without it, you will die. Would this doctor be guilty of basing his or her decision only on opinion or of holding to a worldview regardless of the proven efficacy of the treatment? Of course not. The proof of the truth that treatment works is in the people who had the treatment and lived and those who refused it and died.

The effects of evil and sin are present within this world for anyone to see. The nature of God's goodness is also plainly visible for all to observe. Jesus Christ came to demonstrate the goodness of God in defeating and eradicating evil, sin, and death. Many people are ignorant of this truth. Therefore, it is up to us teachers to help them connect the dots, to help them see the Creator and Sustainer in the world, to understand that He is a personal God who loves them, and to share the good news of Jesus Christ, the Master Teacher. As we teach truth to our students, we are sharing the gospel. We must be bold as we communicate truth to the students entrusted to us and defend it against all challenges.

Chapter 3 discussion questions are the following:
1. How would you answer Pilate's question: "What is truth?"
2. How have you seen the foundation of objective truth errors and undermined?
3. In the subject(s) that you teach, how have you seen the truth of God displayed?
4. Describe how you perceive yourself as a defender of truth.

CHAPTER 4

COMMUNICATION

Imagine if you were responsible to teach a large group of people. This group is not just a few hundred but a multitude of thousands. To this task, add the challenges of having to teach outdoors with the ambient sounds: the wind, the drone of people, and the incessant lapping of waves against the shore where you stand. It is vitally important that you speak to everyone present with clarity and presence but without any electronic amplification devices or presentation tools. How would you handle it?

Jesus faced this very scenario as He taught a large crowd on the banks of the Sea of Galilee. The Gospel of Mark recounts that the crowd was so large that Jesus got into a boat and pushed it out onto the water so He might teach all gathered to hear Him (Mark 4:1–2). At first reflection, teaching from a boat might seem to have been merely a necessity to keep from being hemmed in since the eager crowd pressed in around Him. While this is certainly a contributing factor for Jesus's getting into a boat, another more pivotal reason is clear: He placed Himself on the water so His voice would carry better to the gathered crowd and assure that all could view Him.

Consider the genius of the Master Teacher in this scenario. Sound travels much better over water than it does land. So speaking while on the water ensured His audience could hear Him. Additionally, the bank surrounding the lake where Jesus taught sloped up from the water level creating a natural amphitheater. This strategy was an incredibly innovative approach to teaching the multitude that had gathered to hear Jesus instruct them in the truth.

Challenges in Communication

It is easy to read the accounts in the gospels of Jesus's teaching and not consider the strategies He used to effectively communicate His message. We are tempted to assume that these occasions were too ethereal to be impaired by the challenges posed to anyone teaching outdoors. I often imagine the times Jesus taught as depicted in scenes from movies—a serene environment free from all distractions that would hinder communication. This was not the case.

A careful reading of the gospels reveals that Jesus faced the nitty-gritty challenges every teacher of His time did. As we noted, crowds often pressed in around Him straining to see and hear Him. We read accounts of people climbing trees and descending through roofs just to see Him (see Luke 19:1–9; Mark 2:1–13). Everywhere Jesus went, those seeking truth and healing followed Him, as did those who sought to discredit Him. Jesus faced as much interference in His attempts to teach as any modern educator. Yet He continually adapted both to His surroundings and to the needs of His listeners to communicate the truth of God.

As the Son of God, could Jesus have miraculously made His voice boom over all distractions with such a display that it would have compelled all to hear Him? True, He did perform miracles: raised people from the dead, ordered those who were diseased and disabled to be well, and gave sight back to the blind. With only His voice, He even commanded a storm to dissipate. Even so, the Bible never mentions an instance when Jesus used miracles to enhance His presentation. He used miracles mainly to authenticate His message that He was the Son of God sent to teach truth and save the lost. Why would He not use miracles to overcome distractions?

As we have already seen, when Jesus taught, He did so within the limitations of His human body and the cultural framework of

His day. The Master Teacher did this for one simple reason: to underscore the reality that He was human.

In His letter to the Christians in Ephesus, the Apostle Paul praised Jesus for emptying Himself of His glory and becoming a man (Philippians 2:5–11). This central biblical doctrine, also known as the kenosis, reveals how Jesus serves as the link between God's holiness and sinful humanity. In examining the role of Jesus as the Master Teacher, we must never forget one vital characteristic of who He was: a fully human man who was also fully God. Just as Jesus chose to empty Himself of His glory and submit to the limitations of being a man, He also allowed Himself to teach within the confines of any mortal rabbi.

Overcoming Student Distractions

Our students are distracted. We see it in our classrooms every day. No matter how interesting we try to make our lessons or how dynamic we present them, we will always have distracted students. Studies show that students are distracted more now than ever before. This is not surprising.

One culprit of this distraction is the misuse (or rather overuse) of technology. Flickering smartphones and tablets vie for students' attention. Television, movies, internet videos, social media, and video games offer quick and easy entertainment. This technology is not inherently bad, but students (and many adults, myself included) often abuse it. Technology plays a vital role in education, but some distractions are harmful to our students.

Most distractions are internal rather than external. The distractions we see in our classrooms are only a small part of what is present within the students. The vast majority of what diverts our students is what they bring within them when they darken our classroom doors. Within their hearts and minds are intricate collections of emotions, hopes, dreams, concerns, fears, and disappointments. Our students are magnets in which everything they see and hear attaches to them. If their experiences are mainly good, they will act according to the goodness attached to them. Yet if our students have suffered from cruelty, neglect, apathy, and other evils, they will likewise act accordingly.

Kids carry more burdens than we adults assume. Young people often feel more strongly and hurt more deeply than what we perceive. Even students who seem emotionally well-adjusted can bottle up large amounts of hurt and anxiety. Ultimately, the condition of their hearts plays an important role in their ability to learn truth.

The Master Teacher acknowledged the impact the condition of the heart has on a learner. Consider His parable of the sower in Mark 4:1–20.

In this parable, the sower broadcasts seeds, representative of the manner in which Christian teachers communicate truth. The seed falls onto different types of soil, which are like the hearts and minds of students; some of which are so hardened that they are not able to learn. Some hearts and minds are like the rocky ground. They learn but not to the full measure because their growth is stunted. Finally, many of our students' condition is like the ground covered with thorns. Inasmuch as they are capable of learning, the distractions in their lives choke their full ability to learn and grow. Our goal is to cultivate the hearts and minds of our students so that they can grow and flourish.

The Master Teacher's parable offers a strategy to reach students who struggle to learn because of internal distractions. If our students' hearts and minds are uncultivated, rocky, or riddled with thorns, we must adopt the mindset of a gardener and do what we can to provide our students with everything they need to receive the seeds of truth and understanding.

Whether the seeds take root and thrive is not up to us. It is God's business. Our job is to be diligent in our work of preparing our students' hearts and minds. We must sow truth, tend to our students' needs as best we can, and encourage them to grow by weeding out any hindrances knowing that God alone makes their hearts and minds increase. Just as a gardener is limited to preparing the soil and then depends on the rain and sunshine to make the seed grow, a teacher is limited to preparing their students then watches for God to bring their talents and intellect to bloom. Renowned Christian educator C. S. Lewis understood a teacher's role when he stated: "The task of the modern educator is not to cut down jungles, but to irrigate deserts."[22]

A word of warning: helping our students carry these burdens is a tiring task. It will take a toll. Within the United States, more than 41 percent of teachers will leave the profession within the first five years.[23] Factors researchers cite for this premature exodus of educators include large classes, high-stakes standardized testing, administrative issues, and student behavior.

The deck seems stacked against teachers. At times, even the most stalwart educators are tempted to buckle under these challenges. From the numerous conversations I have had with teachers who have either left the profession or are seriously considering it, an additional factor emerged: the overwhelming feeling of hopelessness they experience when faced with the needs of their students.

Normally, this feeling appears when teachers isolate themselves from other teachers or when they fail to share their concerns with another understanding educator. Guard yourself against this feeling of hopelessness. Remind yourself that it takes a team to help students succeed. Find a seasoned teacher to mentor you. At the very least, team with a fellow teacher and carry each other's burdens. King Solomon, the most famous teacher of ancient Israel, offered this same advice: "Iron sharpens iron, so one man sharpens another" (Proverbs 27:17 NASB).

The Power of Questions

The average teacher asks one question per minute while teaching. That is approximately 360 questions a day or over 67,000 per academic year. Teachers are in the business of asking questions. There is a good reason for this. Asking questions is an essential part of effective communication. Educational researcher Guy Claxton described the power of asking questions in the classroom: "Good learning starts with questions, not answers."[24]

Questions are powerful tools for both students and teachers. Asking questions is a natural byproduct of the learning process. When encountering a new subject or when students do not understand a concept, they ask for clarification or explanation. This is desirable since it helps them advocate for their own learning. However, many students do not ask the right kinds of questions.

In classical education, the practice of asking questions to gain clarity and derive answers based on a presupposition is called the Socratic method. This didactic style, championed by the Greek philosopher Socrates, consists of a series of questions asked in sequence to deduce the clearest and most concise answer possible. This methodology has been a cornerstone for classical Western education for millennia. Its endurance throughout the centuries underscores the power and value of questioning in education.

In essence, effective questions are those that go beyond simple yes or no answers. They are questions that require the students to think critically about a matter in order to explain how the answer interconnects with their own experience and the truth of the world around them. As we have already established, it is the job of the teacher to communicate truth to their students. One of the most powerful ways to do this is by engaging students in asking the right kinds of questions as they encounter the truth God has equipped them to learn.

Jesus loved to ask questions. An examination of His teaching style uncovers His reliance upon questioning to communicate truth. Herman Horne remarked that when we study the way the Master Teacher used questions, "we are near the heart of the teaching method of Jesus."[25]

The gospels record Jesus asking a wide variety of questions. He asked both open- and close-ended questions and rhetorical and nonrhetorical. The Master Teacher asked some questions to make a connection with others (see Mark 2:8, 5:30; Luke 8:30, 8:45; John 1:38). He asked other questions to propel the minds and hearts of His hearers to consider the truth of His teachings (see Matthew 11:6, 16:15, 16:26; John 5:44, 8:10, 21:16; just to name a few).

As Jesus demonstrated, asking questions is a powerful tool to help the teacher perceive how well the students understand a concept. Questions can also provide students a frame upon which they can build their knowledge from basic comprehension to more complex.

In asking questions, Jesus changed the world. If we are to communicate the truth of the world He made, we too must ask the right questions. In His humility, Jesus offered us the perfect example of communication in an imperfect world. He subjected Himself to hindrances and stubborn hearts so we could witness our Master Teacher at work. We will never communicate as effectively as He did; He does not expect us to do so. But we can communicate truth by following His example. When we do, we will be effective communicators. More important, we will honor Christ, our Master Teacher.

The Power of Story

I once overheard a little girl in a Sunday school class make an astute observation. After hearing a parable of Jesus, she said, "Wow! Jesus was a good storyteller!" This is a wonderful title for the Master Teacher.

People love stories. Familiar characters who face challenges similar to our own intrigue us. As we discover what happens to these characters, we wonder how we would act in similar circumstances. We also bring to light a deeper understanding buried within us. Stories have a tendency to help us see ourselves in a stronger light, especially stories that teach us the truth of God. To borrow an analogy from the Apostle Paul, our perception of ourselves is like looking into a mirror in a dim room (see 1 Corinthians 3:12). When the light of God's truth illuminates the mirror, we can truly see ourselves.

Stories have a way of revealing God's truth because precepts, truths, and ideas are embodied in them, reflecting our own experiences. Take any abstract or hard-to-understand concept; place it within a story, and it becomes clear and compelling.

The Master Teacher knew this, and He made good use of it. One-fourth of all the words found in the four gospels (Matthew,

Mark, Luke, and John) are the moral stories Jesus told, known as parables.

The synoptic gospel writers (Matthew, Mark, and Luke) used the Greek word for parable (*parabolē*) about fifty times. The etymology of this Greek word comes from the root word *paraballō*—a compound word comprised of *para* (meaning "next to" or "alongside") and *ballein* ("to throw"). It is a beautiful example of figurative language. The idea behind this term is of an abstract idea or precept that is thrown alongside a story for the sake of clarity.[26]

Jesus often communicated the truth of God by throwing it alongside a story. Jesus used this teaching method so often that He drew back the curtain for His disciples so they would know why.

> Therefore, I speak to them in parables; because while seeing they do not see, and while hearing they do not hear, nor do they understand. (Matthew 13:13 NASB)

Jesus knew His audience. They were a hard-hearted bunch guilty of spiritual blindness. By offering truth in an easily understood yet compelling format, Jesus revealed the deep reality of God to a shallow audience. It was a divine act of kindness. In the Master Teacher, we have holy God who is reaching down to ignorant, sinful humans so that they can know God and be saved. This reflects the dynamic nature of Jesus's parables: they grow deeper as the believer matures. They are simple and direct enough to offer a spark of understanding in the uninformed but then, in the seasoned believer, set ablaze and illuminate comprehension of the deeper things of God.

We can be effective communicators by following the example of the Master Teacher. Utilizing stories and illustrations, we can help our students better learn. If Jesus relied on this form of communication to impart the truth of God, we would do well to follow His example.

Chapter 4 discussion questions are the following:
1. What hindrances to communication have you encountered?

2. How have you overcome these distractions?
3. How have you used the power of questions in your classroom?
4. Describe how you have used the power of stories in your classroom?

CHAPTER 5

LEADERSHIP

When you think of a leader, who do you envision? What characteristics does this person possess? What actions or behaviors does he or she demonstrate? What mental pictures are conjured in your mind? Someone who is a trendsetter? Someone who stands apart from the crowd, offering guidance and wisdom? Perhaps a better question is, in your own experience, whom do you regard as a leader? The chances are good that the person you are thinking of is or was a teacher in some capacity.

Teachers are leaders.

Dr. Albert Mohler said it best: "Every great leader is a great teacher, and the greatest leaders seize every opportunity to teach well."[27] Because of the nature of their role, teachers have the responsibility to lead and influence their students. This is true for both secular and Christian teachers. However, the Christian teacher possesses a more sacred and weighty charge over their students.

The Christian Educational Leader

As a Christian educator, you are a leader. However, your calling as a Christian educational leader is different from a secular teacher because you have the honor to lead your students under the authority of Jesus Christ. God has allowed you to be a valuable link between your students and Him.

The chain of command is simple: you, the teacher, follow Christ, and your students follow you. The Apostle Paul encouraged those in the Corinthian church, who were placed under his instruction, to obey this same paradigm: "Be imitators of me, as I am of Christ" (1 Corinthians 11:1). You are the compass that sets the course for your students. They mimic the virtues you exhibit and understand the world around them through your leadership. Therefore, your primary job is to follow the leadership of the Lord Jesus Christ and, by your example, demonstrate to your students how they are to also follow Him.

This hierarchy challenges a presupposition many people have about leaders. Often a leader is thought to have no one above them. Like the captain of a ship to whom the crew answers, there is no other authority. There is one leader, and the rest are followers. In one, and only one, sense this is true. God is the head and ultimate authority of all that exists. He does not have a superior. However, everything in creation is meant to follow His leadership. Either we are corrupted by our willful refusal to follow His leadership or we eternally thrive as we submit our wills to God. The New Testament epistles lend their voices to the role of leadership and how it ought to be understood in light of God's authority. Their harmonious message centers on the hierarchy of leadership under God and to the fact that every leader is answerable to God's authority.

It does not matter the capacity in which you teach or the age of your students, some under your leadership have never seen the example of a Christ-led life. This honor is given to you. Whether you teach kindergarten students the fundamentals of reading or challenge a doctoral student's thesis, you are called to exhibit the qualities of Christ to your students.

Being Christ-imitating educators to our students does not require us to proselytize everyone who sets foot in our classroom. Many of us who work in public education would most assuredly lose our jobs if we adopted this tactic. Instead, we must utilize the strategy Jesus commanded when He encouraged His followers to "let your light shine before others, that they may see your good deeds and glorify your Father in heaven" (Matthew 5:16 NIV). Our words and deeds must underscore our confession of faith in Jesus Christ even when we are unable to verbally profess it.

Throughout His ministry, the Master Teacher consistently pointed out that His work was to glorify His heavenly Father. By His example, Jesus provided the trajectory we are to follow. There is no retreat for the Christian educator, no half-measures. We are called to be servants of God and leaders of people for the purpose of showing them the way to God.

How are we to accomplish this?

Again, we look to Jesus's life for our answer. As a leader, Jesus was also a servant (see Philippians 2:7; Isaiah 42:1); therefore, we must be servants.

Keep in mind that we are leaders because we are servants. In a broad sense, this notion is easy to understand. All teachers strive to serve the common good of students and society alike. We serve our students by instructing and guiding them, and in turn, we serve society by preparing future generations. However, the richer meaning for the Christian educator comes from the understanding of our place within God's order. We are His servants who are called to serve our students. Our goal is not simply to offer knowledge and understanding of impersonal forces or concepts existing within the universe. It is to reveal the personality and love of the God who created the universe. This truth is best taught when our students see it in our lives. God made it that way.

He desired His followers, His disciples, to lead not only with words but with godly actions. Why? So that we represent Jesus Christ to others. We are to show our students who Christ is. The Apostle Paul underscored our task this way: "We are ambassadors for Christ, God making His appeal through us. We implore you on behalf of Christ, be reconciled to God" (2 Corinthians 5:20).

Teachers are well-situated to exhibit true servant leadership. Serving is innately ingrained within our profession. Embracing this realization and dedicating our actions to honor the Master Teacher empower us to be the most dynamic and successful teachers possible.

Trials of a Christian Leader

Following the example of Jesus Christ as an educational leader does not mean that we will always enjoy success and never experience failure. Nor does it guarantee that others will not accuse and blame us when things go belly up. On the contrary, being a Christian educational leader ensures that we will certainly experience criticism, blame, and even failure. I offer three main reasons why we will face such trials.

The first reason is due to our own nature. We are sinful and imperfect. We will make mistakes. It is not a matter of if we will fail but when. And for many of us (myself included), we will fail frequently. Therefore, sometimes we deserve to be criticized and blamed. In those instances, we should own up to our failures, acknowledge our mistakes, confess what we did wrong, and try to make them right. As simplistic and, perhaps, even childish as this sounds, it is the exact prescription many of us need. Many people ignore this fundamental practice of self-evaluation and self-correction. Like children caught doing something wrong, we want to pretend it was not our fault and try to pass on the blame to someone or something else.

Many religious teachers Jesus encountered erred in this way. This group of teachers, known collectively as the scribes and Pharisees, found fault in others without looking at their own shortcomings. They made this mistake when they encountered Jesus. The Master Teacher gave them such a rebuke that they limped back to their sanctimonious practices.

> Woe to you, scribes and Pharisees, hypocrites! For you are like whitewashed tombs which on the outside appear beautiful, but inside they are full of dead men's bones and all uncleanness. So you, too, outwardly appear righteous to men, but inwardly you are full of hypocrisy and lawlessness. (Matthew 23:27–28)

Jesus made an insightful accusation in this rebuke when He called the scribes and Pharisees "hypocrites." A hypocrite was a theatrical term known in the Hellenistic world for someone who was an actor or pretender. Ancient Greek playwrights such as Xenophon and Aristophanes used this term to describe actors who performed in their plays.[28] Jesus used it in the negative sense as someone who condemns others for their sins while pretending they are free of any wrongdoing.

The Master Teacher radiantly displayed His role as a leader. He did not shirk from speaking the truth. The scribes and Pharisees were well-known among the people and in the established order of the Jewish educational system, but that did not stop Christ's boldness. Leadership does not mean following the status quo to maintain a system; it is fearlessly speaking truth to all levels of power. But, and here is the caveat, in doing so, we must be careful not to be hypocrites in the process. We honor the Master Teacher when we recognize our shortcomings, confess our sins, seek His forgiveness, and lean into His grace.

The second reason leaders are sure to face criticism and blame is for the simple fact that leaders will always experience pushback. It is a basic human reaction to look for someone to blame when things do not go as desired. When people are dissatisfied with something, they look for a scapegoat. Those in leadership are easy targets and will face the full brunt of disgruntlement from many people. Sometimes, their accusations are warranted; other times, they are not. Regardless, criticism is to be expected.

The third reason we face opposition is unique to the Christian educational leader. As we teachers strive to imitate Christ, the supernatural opposition to the Christian message by society and culture (what the Bible calls "the world") confront us. The Master Teacher, himself, warned us:

> If the world hates you, know that it has hated me
> before it hated you. If you were of the world, the
> world would love you as its own; but because you
> are not of the world, but I chose you out of the

world, therefore the world hates you. Remember
the word that I said to you: "A servant is not
greater than his master." If they persecuted me,
they will also persecute you. If they kept my
word, they will also keep yours. (John 15:18–20)

Did you notice the crux of Jesus's warning? If we follow His
example and imitate Him in our role as educational leaders, we are
sure to experience hardships and a variety of trials from those who
are hostile to Christ's teachings. As we previously explored, that is
not to say that every problem or hardship we encounter is a direct
confrontation from evil, supernatural forces. Even if they are not due
to spiritual attacks, they are a direct result from serving in a world
that is corrupted and dying from sin.

As we explored in chapter 3, what the New Testament calls "the
world" is enemy-occupied ground. Satan, the fallen angel who led
the rebellion against God, occupies this world and seeks to encourage human rebellion against God. When the Master Teacher came
to the earth, He came to establish His church as a movement of
truth, empowered by His grace, to combat the evil works of Satan.
As Christians, we are enlisted to fight against this spiritual assault on
God's goodness and truth. Christian teachers are some of the most
important warriors in this war, but we must understand the battle-
field of how "the world" operates.

In his letter to fellow Christians, the apostle John expounds
upon the idea of how the world opposes, and even hates, Christ and
His followers:

Do not love the world or the things in the world.
If anyone loves the world, the love of the Father
is not in him. For all that is in the world—the
desires of the flesh and the desires of the eyes and
pride of life—is not from the Father but is from
the world. (1 John 2:15–17)

The theme of love laced throughout both the gospel and epistles of John demonstrates, by comparison, the reality that to love God is to hate the evil of the world. Specifically, to love God is to hate "the lust of the flesh, the lust of the eyes, and the boasting of life" that permeates all worldly systems, including education. These three offenses are the perversion of the virtues of properly enjoying the physical world through our bodily senses, appreciating the beauty and orderliness God created, and praising the worth of God before oneself.

These virtues are what Christian teachers must bestow to their students in both what they say and how they live in order to overcome the world. Here again, we find how God intended for His truth to be communicated through teachers living out a godly example. Students will not learn virtue by being only told what it is; they must see it.

Leading through Virtue

Virtue is powerful. It is effective in combating the world because at the core of the Christian virtues is love, specifically, the love of God. We love God and practice virtue when we reject all perversions and, by His grace, live the way He desires while teaching others to do likewise. This continual process of rejecting evil, embracing the goodness of God, and instructing our students on how to do the same is the utmost calling of a Christian teacher and the highest aim of true education.

Here is where the core purpose of education begins to shift and transform in modern minds. Many teachers regard imparting knowledge as the main purpose of the educator. In reality, this is only of secondary importance. Virtue, as the Bible reveals it, is the most important concept a teacher can impart. Knowledge is only a vehicle that ferries wisdom, truth, and virtue.

Of course, that is not to say knowledge is not important. Indeed, it is vitally important. However, it does not surpass the overarching necessity of virtue. Our culture is so deep within the mire of moral subjectivism that I must clarify an important point. I am not speaking of the paltry, substitutive excuse that we will call "subjective virtue." This is the belief that people can behave in any way that pleases them, and by the sheer fact that they choose to act accordingly makes it their own "virtue." "Live your own truth" is a common refrain heard in our culture. Following this course of thought at any length soon reveals the flaws of any such personal philosophy. Prisons are full of people who decided to follow their own "truths" that were contrary to rightful laws.

Subjectivism fails from a historical perspective. Humans have always understood the role of education as not only teaching right from wrong but also embracing goodness while rejecting evil. Many writers and scholars of the early church age observed this point. They regarded the Greek philosophers as proof that even those without direct divine revelation through the Holy Scriptures understood the indivisible nature of knowledge and virtue.

Two such giants of Greek philosophy, Plato and his student Aristotle, both revealed that the ultimate value of education is not the amassing of facts and knowledge but the ability to determine right from wrong. Aristotle said the purpose of education is "to make the student like and dislike what he ought."[29] Likewise, Plato observed that the "object of education is to teach us to love what is beautiful."[30] The philosophical themes of parsing right from wrong and disciplining the evil desires in humans weakly echo the process of the Christian teacher. It is void of the only possible force that empowers a person to live a virtuous life: the loving grace of God.

Plato, Aristotle, and many secular teachers are recipients of God's "common grace." Theologically speaking, common grace is grace God gives all people to observe and learn through natural revelation. The secular teacher, whether he or she knows it or not, works from God's common grace and strives to support and teach ethics that they see as derived from human culture alone. For example, God's common grace direct these teachers to forbid their students to cheat on their classwork. The only basis from which they place this prohibition is on a perceived secular humanistic ethic, but at the root, it is derived from God's common grace. To them, there is no higher authority or standard that cheating violates. To cheat is to go against the majority view of all humans who live in a society.

As the Christian professor and apologist C. S. Lewis illuminated, there is a code of conduct that God has instilled within every person. Therefore, it is evident in reflected to some degree in every culture and civilization that has ever existed.[31] Common virtues are useful to assuring that human society survives. God, through His special grace, has revealed virtues by which humans are allowed to eternally thrive in His holiness.

God's special grace, sometimes called saving grace, is the grace God extends to people who come to faith in Christ and are saved by His sacrifice. By this grace, Christians understand the truth that through Jesus, they can live a virtuous life by loving God.

The Christian teacher operates from God's special grace. As such, it is the responsibility of the Christian leader to align with this special grace by teaching virtue in response to God's holiness. We begin to discover God's holiness when we understand that everyone is sinful. We were all created with the potential to bear the image of God, but through sin, we have been marred and disfigured. Our corruption due to sin is so complete that we have no right to any relationship with the perfect, holy God. However, God's love for us, as damaged and helpless to right ourselves as we are, is so great that He provided His own Son to take the punishment for our ungodliness.

Jesus, God's Son and our Master Teacher, loved His students so much that He gave His life for us. This demonstration of special grace is the absolute example of a leader. The Master Teacher has empowered us with virtue through love. As Christian educational leaders, we are called to serve our students by teaching them the virtues our Savior constantly displayed. By His grace, we must seek to be like Him and allow the Holy Spirit to fill us. The Apostle Paul describes the virtues that grow from a person who has the Holy Spirit:

> But the fruit of the Spirit is love, joy, peace, patience, kindness, goodness, faithfulness, gentleness, self-control; against such things there is no law. And those who belong to Christ Jesus

have crucified the flesh with its passions and desires. If we live by the Spirit, let us also keep in step with the Spirit. (Galatians 5:22–25)

We can lead by virtue only when we recognize the depths of love our Master Teacher has in sacrificing His life for us as well as the Holy Spirit dwelling in us, growing in our love for God, and sharing the virtues, "fruit of the Spirit," that is cultivated in our lives by God's grace. Then and only then we will be complete leaders.

Chapter 5 discussion questions are the following:
1. What successes and failures have you experienced as a leader?
2. How have you resisted your calling as a Christian educational leader?
3. How would your student and/or other teachers describe your role as a leader?
4. What virtues would your students and/or other educators say they see in how you lead?

CHAPTER 6

LOVE AND COMPASSION

The file folder fell to the table with a loud thud. Its heft was due to the nearly two inches of incident reports, disciplinary notices, and other documents about the student who would soon be mine. Leafing through the documents, I came across reports of this young person inflicting harm on teachers, ranging from broken thumbs to a concussion. The principal assured me of her confidence that I could handle this student.

I was not so sure.

To say that the first couple of weeks with my new student were difficult would be an understatement; they were terrible. At first, the only times he even acknowledged my presence was when he became angry and zeroed in on me as his target. I often went home with scratches, cuts, and bruises all over my hands and forearms along with torn sleeves and shirt pockets.

If there was ever a time when I was tempted not to love a student, or anyone for that matter, this was it. Of course, I understood that most of his tantrums were due to his condition, and I tried to empathize with him. But when he hit, kicked, slapped, pinched, scratched, and even spat upon me day after day, the idea of loving the offender was far from my mind.

Love

It is a difficult lesson every teacher must learn from an issue we have all faced. Reminisce with any teacher for any length of time, and the topic of challenging students will inevitably arise. We have all faced unlovable students—those who dance on our last nerve. They know the buttons to push and, unknowingly or not, they push them. They are the rocks in our shoes. At first, we might seem immune to their annoying conducts that are on an obvious campaign to take us teachers out.

No doubt the images of a few students have popped into your mind.

We all know it is difficult to love a student who opposes you. But when we are daily challenged or even attacked, the last thing we want is to attempt any positive interactions with these rascals.

That is certainly how I have felt. Whenever I was faced with the challenge to love someone who acted so unlovable, I questioned what it meant to love my students or anyone for that matter. How was I to define love, let alone practice it, in such a challenging situation?

Let's begin by stating the obvious. As Christians, we are commanded to love others. This is the hallmark of any Christian. As Christian teachers, that means we ought to love our students—all of them. One of Jesus's disciples, John, encouraged Christians to let their love shine to all as evidence that they belong to God.

> Beloved, let us love one another, for love is from God, and whoever loves has been born of God and know God. Anyone who does not love does not know God, because God is love. In this the love of God was made manifest among us, that God sent His only Son into the world, so that we might live through Him. In this is love, not that we loved God but that He loved us and sent His Son to be the propitiation for our sins. Beloved, if God so loved us, we also ought to love one another. (1 John 4:7–11)

In short, because God commands us to love, we do not get to choose whether or not to love others. Likewise, we do not get to choose whether or not to love our students. Thankfully, this mandate to love does not rely on our own initiative and ability. The impetus is fully on Jesus. Along with the command to love, He offers the example of how to love and empowers us to love.

When Jesus was asked to state the greatest of all the commands of God, He replied with a twofold command: "You shall love the Lord your God will all your heart and with all your soul and with all your mind and with all our strength... You shall love your neighbor as yourself" (Mark 12:30–31).

The order of this dual command is important. We must love God first then love others as we love ourselves. Perhaps upon reading this command, you do not see how it is God who empowers us to love. Once again, the Apostle John comes to our aid by revealing that the only reason we can love is because God loved us first even when we were as unlovable as our tough students (see 1 John 4:19).

God made all humans in His image. This is evident in our ability to give and receive love. However, since our condition is completely wrecked by sin, we are not able to love the way God intended. We can only do so when we first seek to love God—the source of love. This is where we must start. If we are to love our students (or anyone else), we must love God first.

Loving God is not to be a means to an end. We should not desire to love God just to be empowered to love others. That is not true love. Loving our fellow humans is a wonderful endeavor in which God may use to guide us to what we are ultimately created to do: to love Him. But I do not want to mislead anyone. Loving God is the primary reason we were created.

Here, an obvious challenge presents itself. How can we, as riddled with sin as we are, love God? How can corrupted humans love a perfect God? The short answer is, on our own, we cannot. Although we are designed to love God, we are marred and incapable of doing so. We are like shattered vases no longer able to fulfill their purposes. Here is where we begin to discover the depths of God's love. While we were dead in our love of God, unable to love Him, He loved us.

He provided a means through His Son to restore us so that we might love Him, and in loving Him, we can rejoin our created purpose.

We have the honor of sharing the love of God with our students. Let me clarify. We are not sharing *our* love for our students, but God is sharing His love through us in our dealings with our students. This can only take place when we love God above everyone and everything in our lives.

The Master Teacher loved like this. He loved His heavenly Father beyond anything or anyone else. This love brought Him to the corrupted world where He took on flesh and bone. This love made Him the Master Teacher. This love led Him to the cross to die a torturous death. Also, this love raised Him from the dead. This is the love we have the honor of communicating to our students.

Sharing the love of God with our students is a process. None of us love perfectly. And even though we have determined to love as Christ loved, we will not learn to do so quickly.

Some practical advice might be in order at this point. Loving others does not necessitate we are always happy or have warm feelings toward them. This misunderstanding stems from believing our feelings are the indicator of the degree to which love is present within us: the stronger the feeling of affection, the greater the presence of love. Conversely, the lack of such positive feelings is proof of the absence of love.

The way we feel is a false guide to our understanding of love. Puritan writer Richard Sibbes encouraged his readers not to measure God's love by their own feelings: "The sun shineth as clearly in the darkest day as it does in the brightest. The difference is not the sun, but in some clouds which hinder the manifestation of the light thereof."[32]

We will experience times of not feeling like loving our students. In our weakest moments, we might brand them as "unlovable" and find no cause to show them love or compassion. Such feelings should not be ignored, but neither should they be acted upon without first reminding ourselves that our students are loved by God and created in His image. As such, they are to be loved by those who follow the Son of God just as He loves us. In doing so, we fully represent Jesus

Christ to those who may not know Him. You could very possibly be the only example of Christ your students have witnessed and the example they remember when presented with the gospel message.

A key practical approach in loving others when we don't feel like it is to realize that to love someone in this manner is a matter of the will. Place your feeling aside and determine to treat that person in a loving and kind way. The more you treat someone lovingly, you will find that you have developed a love for them that is not reliant on a feeling. Remember, the Master Teacher never commanded His followers to maintain a loving feeling. He made loving others their duty and life's work.

Loving God through Teaching

Perhaps one of the greatest discoveries we can make as teachers is that we can honor and love God in our profession. Everything we do as we work in our school buildings and classrooms five days a week from August to June could be an act of loving God and honoring Him with our work.

In the closing remarks of his first letter to the Corinthians, Paul offers a brief but profound exhortation: "Let all that you do be done in love" (1 Corinthians 16:14). This is a simple and poignant command with major reverberations. When we apply this command in our roles as teachers, we will find renewed vigor and purpose in our work.

To love others the way Jesus commanded honors God. It is the mark of a follower of Christ and the proof that we are students, or disciples, of the Master Teacher. While teaching, Jesus declared to His followers:

> A new commandment I give to you, that you love one another: just as I have loved you, you also are to love one another. By this all people will know that you are my disciples, if you have love for one another. (John 13:34–35)

Teaching can be an act of worship. When Christian teachers follow the command of the Master Teacher and love their students as Jesus first loved us, we honor God. The realization of this truth has the power to transform us as educators. We will face very difficult students. We will have some we cannot on our own truly love. But Christ has loved us to empower us to love others for His glory. When we Christian teachers love our students the way Jesus intends, we honor and love our Master Teacher.

Even in the mundane activities of our careers, we have the opportunity to honor and worship God. While it is never too late in your teaching career to embrace God's command to love, if you are a student preparing for a career in education, you can begin now to share the love of God with your fellow students and professors. I like what St. Bernard of Clairvaux said on this matter:

> There are those who seek knowledge for the sake
> of knowledge; that is Curiosity. There are those
> who seek knowledge to be known by others; that
> is Vanity. There are those who seek knowledge in
> order to serve; that is Love."[33]

Throughout our teaching careers, we will find ways to honor God. These opportunities are obvious in the big things: seeing prayers answered for a student or when students return after a few years to thank us for influencing them. We rejoice in and thank God because we cannot help but see His work in those big moments.

We also seek ways to honor and love God in the little things: the dull lesson preparations, the humdrum meetings, and the endless paperwork; all of these are times to honor Him. Keep in mind what the Master Teacher taught: no matter how insignificant or menial the task might be, if we do it to honor Christ, it is as if we do it for Him (see Matthew 25:42–45).

Embracing every opportunity to love, honor, worship, and serve Christ in our classrooms will transform us. It will dominate the way we interact with our students and fellow educators. We will be the best teachers possible when we submit ourselves to God and become conduits of His love for our students. We have no greater impact on them than this. As Christians, glorifying God is our ultimate purpose. As Christian teachers, we fulfill this purpose as we share His love with our students.

Compassion

Thus far, we have discussed love, but a component to love is compassion. Having established the necessity of loving God before all else, it is now important to understand how we may put into practice loving other humans. The beginning of loving others, especially those who may try us at times, is to have compassion on them, which is the call to action to help others by improving their condition.

Our Master Teacher gives us the template to follow. The New Testament Gospels underscore numerous examples of how Jesus's compassion compelled Him to heal the sick, restore the dead, and teach those who were lost (see Matthew 9:36, 14:14, 15:32, 20:34; Mark 6:34, 8:2–3; Luke 7:13). Often, His compassion is described as the result of His regarding the crowds as "sheep without a shepherd" (see Matthew 9:36)—a people without someone to guide and protect them.

Three of the four gospels, Matthew, Mark, and Luke (known as the Synoptic gospels), record Christ's compassion toward His followers.[34] The Greek verb *splagchnizomai* is used to describe "a deep yearning in one's bowels."[35] The bowels, not the heart, were considered the seat of emotions in the first century. A modern equivalent of this verb could be the phrase "to feel compassion from the depth of your heart." Jesus did not experience passive motivation toward His students. Rather, He felt compassion for them with His whole heart.

I began this chapter confessing my struggle to love certain students I believed to be unlovable. My struggle was partly due to my refusal to have compassion for them. Out of my own frustration and selfishness, I believed they did not deserve it. I had to ask myself some hard questions: Did those people for whom Christ felt compassion deserve it? Were they considered lovable? The answer is no, more or less than any other sinners including you, me, and the sinners we teach. Christ felt compassion on the fallen human race who, since Adam and Eve, has challenged the holiness of God through sin. None of us is worthy of Christ's compassion. Yet He offers it to us because of His great love. Here again, we discover that we can have compassion only through God's provision. We cannot do it alone.

Following the example of Christ is vitally important for the spiritual and mental health of a teacher. All teachers are motivated by the needs of their students. This motivation to help our students reach their potential and discover their place in the world drives our compassion. However, it is possible for teachers to become so focused on helping their students that they neglect their own well-being. They are like candles who consume themselves while giving light to others. As noble as that sentiment sounds, it is not healthy because it is not what God intended.

God never expected us to love or have compassion in our own strength. If we try to do so, we will quickly burn out from a corrupted form of love and compassion. We would do well to remember that we can love and have compassion for others only when we love God first. Again, we rely on the Apostle John to describe this process.

> We love because He first loved us. If anyone says, "I love God," and hates his brother, he is a liar; for he who does not love his brother whom he has seen cannot love God whom he has not seen. And this commandment we have from Him: whoever loves God must also love his brother. (1 John 4:19–21)

By loving God first, we are empowered to love and have compassion on others, especially our students. In truth, it is not we who generate compassion in our hearts; rather, it is God's love flooding into our hearts that empowers us to have compassion. The lavish love of God is never-ending and ensures that the love and compassion we have for others will never be consumed or extinguished. Though we may struggle in our sinful state, God's grace is sufficient to give us all we need to share His love with those who are honored to call students.

Discipline

Loving our students and having compassion on their condition does not mean that we allow them to behave however they wish. Some parts of our society disagree. It is astonishing that many people seem to disagree with this statement. They embrace the idea that to love someone is to allow them to act in any way they choose.

As we have already established when we discussed the necessity of teaching God's truth, any departure from God's law is error, and error always has consequences. But how do we encourage an individual to refrain from making errors, especially those who continually make them?

The first step in practicing discipline is to love our students enough to teach them the truth, including that they must act in accordance with God's law and commands. What we call "tough love," the Bible calls discipline—a key component in loving our students. God, the source of all truth, love, and goodness, has set the precedence of disciplining in love.

> My son, do not reject the discipline of the LORD
> or loathe His reproof, for whom the LORD loves
> He reproves, even as a father corrects the son in
> whom he delights. (Proverbs 3:11–12 NASB)

We discipline (and are disciplined) because of the love God gives to His followers. To make the love involved in discipline clearer, the Bible describes this process in the context of a father and son relationship. Just as a father disciplines His son out of love, so God disciplines those He loves. This is the model we are to follow.

For us to comprehend discipline and how we are to use it, let's look at what it is not. Discipline is not unjust punishment, and it is definitely not mistreatment. It is not cruelty that forces students to behave in a certain way nor is it coercion of the helpless by the strong. We have all heard horror stories of sadistic displays within classrooms, but these are not examples of true discipline and should never be tolerated.

So what is discipline? The English word comes from the Latin word *discipulus* which means "appropriately enough"—a "student." The original concept viewed the role of a student as someone who trained to think or perform a certain way. This process required a joint effort from both the stick and the carrot in the form of rewards and consequences. Discipline is the correction in which expectations and consequences are clearly made known. It is always for the benefit of the one being disciplined and keeps the goal of the restoration of the individual in mind. It is not always pleasant, but its goal is satisfying.

Teachers promote discipline in the classroom by first maintaining a loving and respectful environment. Within this context, teachers clearly convey expectations along with the corresponding rewards for compliance and consequences for defiance. After communicating these key ingredients of classroom discipline, that leaves only one action for teachers: they must follow through with this disciplinary framework. To maintain discipline in our classes, we must faithfully and consistently bestow both rewards and consequences according to the established guidelines.

The more disciplined our students become, the more successes they will enjoy. Our adherence to respectful and loving classroom discipline helps meet a short-term goal of classroom management, but it also benefits our students beyond their time under our influence. Along with giving our pupils the raw building material of facts and knowledge, we can also give them the tools of critical thinking and curiosity. Equally important is that we equip them with the determination to see the job through. They need the blueprints that clearly mark their expectations and the benefits that come from following the plans in order to reach their goal. Psychologist and former teacher James Dobson stated:

> Children...need to be taught self-discipline and responsible behavior. They need assistance in learning how to handle challenges and obligations of living. They must learn the art of self-control. They should be equipped with the

personal strength needed to meet the demands imposed on them by their school, peer group, and later adult responsibilities."[36]

If we love our students, we will discipline them. It will not be easy and will require a good deal of self-discipline on our part. However, the benefits far outweigh the challenges. Most importantly, encouraging discipline honors God to love those entrusted to us just as He first loved us.

Chapter 6 discussion questions are the following:
1. What qualities do you find "unlovable" in other people, especially your students?
2. Describe what it means to love your students.
3. How would your students and/or other teachers describe the love you have for them?
4. How do your students and/or other teachers witness your love for God?

CHAPTER 7

RELATIONSHIPS

"So you're the new teacher, huh?"

I looked up from the box I was unpacking to see a short, stocky sixteen-year-old boy wearing sweat-soaked practice football jersey standing in the doorway. Several Hispanic teenage boys dressed in similar sweaty garb flanked him on both sides. The first day of school was two weeks out. As the teachers were preparing their classrooms, the football coaches were preparing their players out in the hot Texas sun.

"Yeah, that's me. How are you boys doing?" I used a cheerful tone as I scanned my visitors. The only smile in the room was mine.

"Where are you from?" The inquiry came from a much taller youth who stood with his arms folded across his chest.

I explained I had grown up and went to school in a small town (albeit bigger than theirs) about twenty miles down the road. This information did not seem to elicit much enthusiasm or interest from the small crowd gathered at the door of my classroom. It served only to confirm the main thing these boys had already figured out: I was not from around there.

My audience stared blankly at me. I understood their intention. I was the new teacher many of them would soon have, and I was an outsider who needed vetting to see if he would fit in. I continued to answer their questions until their curiosity seemed satisfied. Slowly, one by one, my sweaty inquisitors turned and left my classroom.

Over the following weeks, many of those young men who initiated our association by giving me the third degree began to open up, eventually smiling and jovially talking to me daily. Our relationship progressed to such a point that I was finally able to ask a few of the boys why they had quizzed me so cynically the first time we met.

The boys seemed stunned as if I had just asked the dumbest question they had ever heard.

"You know why, Mr. Wade! It's because you're white. But now you're one of us!"

This was an incredible compliment. I was satisfied to know that I had reached this reluctant group of young men. I had formed a relationship, and as such, I could do my job as a teacher even more effectively.

God with Us

God created humans with the need to form and sustain relationships. We are social creatures who require relationships for survival. Our very existence demands we seek out support, love, and respect. Why did God create us with the need for relationships?

God designed humans to be His image-bearers. All the good things that make God who He is—love, peace, creativity, and the joy of connection with others—are imprinted on each of us. Sin has corrupted our ability to enjoy these characteristics perfectly, but the desire is present. We yearn to be connected with others.

As He has revealed Himself in the Trinity, God is completely satisfied in the relationship the three persons have with one another as the Godhead. God the Father, God the Son, and God the Holy Spirit exist in a perfect trifecta of harmony. God is the perfect example of all a relationship should be. Again, we stumble upon the reality that God is the source of all good, truth, and beauty.

We are made in God's likeness, so we crave relationships that mirror this divine example. Our death sentence of sin prevents us from being in a right relationship with God (for whom our hearts were primarily made) or with other humans. The Master Teacher came to us to restore our relationships.

The first chapter of the gospel of John records one of the most amazing truths about Jesus Christ. Within the opening of his gospel, John describes Jesus as the *Logos*, a Greek term we investigated in chapter 3, the embodiment of God's Word or decree. John describes how Jesus, the Logos, came into the world and "dwelt among us" (John 1:14). The Greek phrase used here literally means that Jesus came to earth and pitched His tent among us.[37] We might say that He moved into the neighborhood.

The implications of this are staggering. Jesus, the very truth of God, God Himself who created everything, came to earth to dwell with humanity. The Apostle Paul further expounds this when he wrote that Jesus "emptied Himself" so He might become part of humanity (see Philippians 2:7).

The holy God, whose rightful place is too splendid and glorious for sinful humanity to comprehend, left His rightful estate and made Himself nothing so He could move in next door. He came to establish a relationship with humanity. He came to our dying and diseased planet and took up the role of Master Teacher.

In order to explore the Christian view of relationships, we must start with the Master Teacher. Born into the human race, Jesus joined a lineage, a family. He had a mother, an adopted father, brothers, and sisters. He had friends and followers. In short, the Son of God had various relationships with the people around Him. God was with them whether they knew it or not.

It is fascinating how God uses familiar human relationships to highlight the close relationship He desires to have with each of us. Jesus, the Son of God, taught that God is our heavenly Father. At salvation, we are born into the family of God as His sons and daughters. We are encouraged to be friends of God. Christians comprise the church which the New Testament describes as the "bride of Christ," a clear reference of the closest context of human relationships—marriage. The relationship that the sacrifice of Jesus Christ grants us is so grand; it requires the totality of human relationships to describe.

The Master Teacher desires a relationship with each of us. He has moved into the neighborhood. His desire is so to lead us into all truth. The most effective manner to accomplish this is to establish a relationship with us. Likewise, we must seek out positive relationships with our students if we are to impart to them all the benefits of God as we teach them.

Establishing Relationships

Positive teacher-student relationships are essential for a successful classroom experience. Until students trust their teachers, the kids will not listen. Without a positive relationship with our students, we come across like the teacher from the *Peanuts* cartoons: a droning "mwa-waa" of incoherent noise. One research study has shown that when teachers purposefully establish strong relationships with their pupils, student academic success improved by 33 percent while their disruptive behavior decreased by 75 percent.[38]

Some teachers, especially new, unconfident ones, seem to struggle with establishing healthy and dynamic relationships with their students. They are usually well-intentioned and wish to have good working relationships with their students. But they struggle to form strong teacher-student relationships.

The first step in connecting with your students is simply to get to know them. This might seem like obvious advice, but many teachers who fail at getting to know their students do not acquaint themselves with their students' personalities, strengths, and weaknesses. Invest the time and effort in getting to know your students, and you will be rewarded with learners who are more attentive, respectful, and successful.

The wheels of the educational process turn more easily when relationships are given priority. Jesus invested in His disciples and recognized their unique characteristics. He even dubbed some of them with nicknames that matched their personalities. He called Simon "Peter" (meaning a "rock"), and He christened James and

John the "sons of thunder" (see Matthew 16:17–18 and Mark 3:17, respectively). Jesus knew His students.

The second step is to change your perception of your role as a teacher. If you are like most teachers (especially those new to the field), you envision your classroom like a well-oiled machine whose gears and cogs work together smoothly and can be programmed to follow your direction. This is never the case. As much as we would like our students to work together without difficulties while following our directions, this does not happen unless we change our approach.

Believing our students must be flexible and conform to our style of teaching will bring you nothing but exasperation. During my first few years of teaching, I was constantly frustrated because I held this faulty view of my students and my role as a teacher. I discovered that when I forged a relationship with my students that included knowing their individual strengths and weaknesses, I was able to adapt my instructional style to accommodate them. Rather than thinking of my classroom as a machine that operated on a given process, I had to know where each student fit in with the whole. Then I could teach accordingly. The result was a far more satisfying and fulfilling teaching-learning experience.

The Bible provides examples of teachers conforming to the needs of their hearers. The grandest example, of course, is the Master Teacher who met humanity where it was so as to transform all who believe in Him for salvation. His students followed His example. Peter lived among the gentiles to understand the mystery of how salvation through Christ was not meant for just the Jews. Paul, who was often the best at encapsulating the role of the Christian in the world, remarked:

> For though I am free from all, I have made myself
> a servant to all, that I might win more of them. To
> the Jews I became as a Jew, in order to win Jews.
> To those under the law I became as one under
> the law (though not being myself under the law)
> that I might win those under the law. To those
> outside the law I became as one outside the law

(not being outside the law of God but under the law of Christ) that I might win those outside the law. To the weak I became weak, that I might win the weak. I have become all things to all people, that by all means I might save some. I do it all for the sake of the gospel, that I may share with them in its blessings. (1 Corinthians 9:19–23)

The process of becoming whatever our students need us to be does not mean that we are relieved of our authority or that we lower our expectations. On the contrary, it heightens both by allowing the light of Christ within us shine so our students can see that we care about them as individuals and that we want them to succeed. As Paul said, we become all things to our students so that "by all means… [we] might save some" (verse 22).

Tuning In

A practical question remains: What is the nuts and bolts approach to getting to know our students and establishing relationships with them?

My dad is an amateur radio enthusiast. Growing up, I spent hours at his side listening to a cacophony of static and signals. I learned from him that if you train your ear long enough, you will pick out radio signals from the noise. With patience and fine-tuning, the signal becomes clearer when you tune into the correct frequency. If we learn to tune into our students, we will discern who they truly are out of the background of noisy interference of negative behavior and distractions. This fine-tuning is what Paul described as becoming "all things to all people."

Allow me to take this illustration a bit further. Most educators view themselves much like a radio station that broadcasts information on a single frequency to many recipients. They believe that it is their job to transmit, and the students' job is to receive the transmission by tuning in to the teacher. If the students fail to receive the signals, they are thought of as either unwilling or unable to learn. On the contrary, educators have the responsibility to tune in to their students' frequencies. Just as my father would tune in to frequencies from all over the amateur radio bands, so must teachers tune and fine-tune their "receivers" to connect to and communicate with their students. Thankfully, this tuning in is not as difficult as it sounds.

I once had a student who returned to my school after having moved away for almost two years. Upon his return, several of the teachers who previously had him in class lamented on his return and warned his current teachers that he was a disrespectful and challenging student. He lived up to this hype!

In dealing with this student, I was frustrated that I could not connect with him. He refused to pay attention in class and was, to no surprise, an incredible distraction. No matter how hard I tried, I could not tune in on my student's frequency. Then I heard that his older sister, who was a previous student of mine, had been diagnosed with a heart condition. The next time I saw my rambunctious student, I pulled him aside to express my concern for his sister and told him that I wanted frequent updates on her condition. At the end of the conversation, I assured him that I would always be available if he needed to talk. The subsequent change in his behavior was startling. Almost immediately, this challenging student became more receptive and willing to put forth an effort in class; all because I had tuned in to his frequency. By showing our students we truly care for them and that we are interested in what is going on in their lives, we can capture their attention and work to defeat their lack of interest in the classroom.

I will not make an overly naïve statement that becoming attuned to our students and seeking to form a relationship with them will solve all of our classroom problems. However, this is the best place to start. The harsh reality is that even after we have connected with our students, there will always be those who seem uninterested, refuse to learn, and shut off themselves. Even the Master Teacher had those who sat under His instruction and still walked away. Teachers can only try to cultivate the hearts and minds of their students and broadcast truth through their relationships with the student. God alone deals with the individuals and causes the work of teachers to bear fruit.

Community

Humans have never had more tools with which to communicate than we do right now. Through technology, you can be alone in a room and still have a connection with the furthest point of the outside world. We have the collective knowledge of humanity available with a few keystrokes or clicks.

Along with the riches of the internet, social media promises connection with people from every area of your life and even beyond. We can send and receive messages, discuss ideas, discover knowledge, and stay in touch with numerous people. With all these available platforms, it is hard to believe anyone could ever lose their sense of community, but it happens often, especially among our students.

Recent research has revealed that although our students are the best-connected generation to exist, a large number of them have lost their sense of community.[39] In fact, they are lonely, proving that access to communication and vast amounts of information do not produce community.

Education produces community. More specifically, education in its basic form—the search for truth—is the progenitor of community life. Consider the most fundamental of communities: small groups of people, or tribes, gathered around a fire. What was the purpose of such a meeting? It was for the transmission of the truth and its application to the world around them. In this elemental transmission of truth, education occurs, and the community is strengthened.

The Master Teacher established the church for this very purpose. He commanded His followers to form groups that would gather together with the purpose of teaching truth and encouraging believers. To continue its mission, the church established schools where the Christian community could grow and impart doctrine to younger generations.

The modern educational system is a direct descendant of the church's mission. Throughout the centuries, the church has established grammar schools, colleges, and universities, many of which are among the most prestigious schools today. As Christianity grew during the first centuries, the need to educate grew with it. By the Middle Ages, most schools were directly run by the church or, in the very least, established by it. As the Bible was translated into the languages of the common people at the dawn of the Protestant Reformation, many leaders of the reformation such as Calvin and Luther advocated the establishment of schools. They believed it was important to create schools where everyone could learn to read, whereby allowing everyone the opportunity to read and study the Word of God. It is clear that Christians have a rich educational history spurred on by the need for Christian community. School would not have been established without the church. As Thomas H. Groome notes, "All of our education efforts will bear little fruit unless they take place within a Christian faith community."[40]

True education and the Christian faith are intertwined and are both important aspects of the church. We can continue the church's mission and offer much-needed community to our students. Once they feel accepted as a valued member of a learning society, our students will flourish into the learners God created them to be.

Relationships are a vital part of education. It begins with the perfect example of the relationship enjoyed by the Trinity. It grows from the relationship Christ offers to His followers, whom He has called, to band together in a community known as the church. Moreover, it is the mission of the church to foster relationships among all humanity through education, first with God and then with other humans.

Chapter 7 discussion questions are the following:
1. Describe your current relationship with Christ.
2. What distractions and interferences have you witnessed in your classroom?
3. How have you "tuned" in to your students?

4. How are you contributing to the sense of community in your classroom/school/church/home/other educational environments?

CHAPTER *8*

INSPIRATION

Discouragement is a harsh enemy to the learning process. It zaps the learner of drive, passion, and self-assurance. It crouches behind every stumble and failure, ready to pounce and destroy any confidence we have in teaching and our students have in learning. It seeks to upset creativity, ambition, perseverance, and hope. Every student will face its melee. The more resilient ones might reel for a time, but they never go down for the count. On the other hand, those who lack the will to overcome these assaults will be deflated and defeated, void of hope and direction.

Does this description seem overly dramatic? It might seem to be, especially if you are feeling encouraged and empowered. But it rings true for anyone who has experienced discouragement. If we are honest with ourselves, we can recall a time when discouragement seized us and threatened not to let go until we identified the source and took steps to remedy the malaise.

However, when young people are hit with discouragement, many of them do not know how to deal with this threat. They cope as best they can. Coping wears many masks, including disruptive behaviors, sullenness, and belligerence. We must strive to inspire and teach them how to conquer discouragement.

Early in my teaching career, I had several students who constantly struggled with bouts of deep discouragement, and as I look back over their time at school, it was no wonder they battled with it.

Many of them were middle-school students who were unable to read at a functional level. They often acknowledged their trouble reading and the frustration they felt. I knew if my students were to experience any success academically, they would first need to overcome their discouragement. In a word, they needed inspiration.

I made each of my students an "Inspiration Folder." To introduce the concept to them, I offered an object lesson depicting the challenge we were facing as a class. I held up an empty balloon and explained to my exasperated pupils how they were like the deflated balloon. They are made to be filled with drive and determination, but because of past failures or lack of knowledge, they were empty; they had not been filled. As I inflated the balloon, I paused at each breath to explain what the breaths represented: making goals (breath), taking chances (breath), celebrating every success no matter how small (breath), and learning from failures (breath). Once the balloon was filled, I held it for the class to see, and I stressed to my students that, in short, they needed to be filled with encouragement. Then I held up an "Inspiration Folder" and told them I had made one for each student in my class. I explained that they were to place their folders on my desk whenever they felt discouraged or overwhelmed. I would write personalized notes of encouragement and return the folders to them.

I was shocked at how often I would find a stack of folders on the corner of my desk. It was not always easy to think of things to write, but the realization that I was expanding my students' belief in their abilities made the trouble worth it.

As the yearly standardized-reading test loomed, I reminded my students to be inspired and filled with high expectations. Three weeks after the test, I received an envelope containing my students' scores. Opening it, I could not believe my eyes. I looked twice to make sure I was reading the scores right. Every student had passed some variation of the standardized test! They had accomplished this goal through hard work and inspiration.

The Master Teacher understood the value of imparting encouragement and inspiration to His disciples. With His imminent separation from His disciples after His resurrection, Jesus knew His students would be tempted to despair. He commanded them to be encouraged by their coming filling with the Holy Spirit. He told them that in the Helper, they would find the fullness of encouragement and inspiration (see John 14:25–27).

Breathing Into

The verb "to inspire" comes from the Latin word *inspirare*, which means to "breathe into" or "infuse."[41] This powerful word picture envisions the infusion of a life-giving force into something, like air into a balloon. To inspire or to be inspired means that where there was once emptiness, now there's fullness. Where there was once death, now there is life. And where there was once desolation, by inspiration, life thrives.

The imagery of God creating Adam from the dust of the earth serves to underscore the scope of inspiration. Once formed, Adam was an empty and lifeless thing, an object presumably with a brain, nerves, bones, and flesh but without the spark of life. It was not until God breathed into his body that Adam came alive. Upon being inspired (quite literally) by God, Adam could think, reason, imagine, feel emotions, and, most important, experience a relationship with God since he was made in the image of God.

Everyone has an innate need to be filled with God-given inspiration. We need the breath of God to fill us, save us from our unworthy state, and bring us back to a right relationship with God. The sacrificial death of the Master Teacher offered the only way this could happen. This sanctifying act was always in view of everything He taught. He is the truth who not only teaches sinful humans what they need but provides the only way they can obtain it.

As teachers who serve Jesus, we are called to be inspirational teachers. Not in the glib sense that the world projects, but in the real manner in which the Master Teacher displayed. God gave our students the gifts of intelligence, curiosity, and reason all wrapped up in the ability to know Him. And in response, we have the joy to be illuminators and mentors to help our students manage their gifts.

This might seem like a daunting task, but like all important matters, God provides us His grace and power to accomplish this most vital goal. Peter reassures us of the power Jesus gives to undertake this task:

> His divine power has granted us all things pertaining to life and godliness through the knowledge of Him who called us to His own glory and excellence, by which He has granted to us His precious and very great promises, so that through them you may become partakers of the divine nature, having escaped from the corruption that is in the world because of sinful desire. (2 Peter 1:3–4)

We have everything we need because we have God's Word, the Scriptures, and His Word is enough. Peter understood that true inspiration and encouragement come only through the divine power revealed in the Bible. God has given us everything we need to pursue godly inspiration and impart it to others through His Word.

Through another apostle, God also gave us practical steps on how we might best inspire our students. In his second letter to Timothy, the Apostle Paul instructs his young protégé on the practical application of Scripture: "All Scripture is breathed out by God and profitable for teaching, for reproof, for correction, and for training in righteousness, that the man of God may be complete, equipped for every good work" (3:16–17).

The phrase *inspired by God* (*theopneustos*) Paul used can be translated as "God-breathed." Its meaning is the same derivation as the Latin term for *inspiration or* "breathing into." The apostle used this word to describe the Scriptures as full of God's inspiration. The apostle commands Christian teachers to build their educational plan upon this firm foundation. No firmer foundation exists since the Word of God is the only all-sufficient source for understanding and inspiration.

With the cornerstone of the Scriptures in place, Paul builds a four-part pedagogical approach by exhorting Timothy to (1) teach, (2) rebuke, (3) correct, and (4) train in righteousness.

The first approach seems obvious since it is the central occupation of every teacher. We must teach. The Greek word Paul uses, *didaskalia* (from which we derive *didactic*), underscores a deeper reality to teaching than the modern understanding of the term "to teach." In the original language, this term largely identified instruction that centered on a specific, objective truth, leaving no room for subjective understanding in this word. That is why several translations of the Bible translate this word simply as "doctrine."

Previously, we have discussed the necessity of teachers to teach the truth of God, or doctrine. Within Paul's exhortation, we encounter the effects of imparting true doctrine: in a word, inspiration.

We witness the effect of people learning biblical doctrine in some of the greatest achievements in human history. From the arts and literature to the social sciences, we have countless examples of how the Word of God has inspired humans to create, compose, write, think, and even govern.

Beethoven composed hundreds of cantatas and orchestral arrangements to communicate the truths of the Bible. Renaissance artists and sculptors competed with themselves to reveal the biblical narrative in a variety of visual forms. Even within the hard sciences, Sir Isaac Newton made great strides in scientific inquiry because his deep biblical convictions inspired him to discover the world God created. These achievements (and countless others from all walks of life throughout history) were accomplished as a direct result of inspiration from the truths of the Bible.

Other than being inspired by the Word of God, a common factor among those who achieved these great discoveries and advancements is that someone took the time to teach them. Inspiration truly comes from teaching according to biblical truth. When we seek to inspire our students in accordance with the Scriptures, we are helping them discover the answers to the big questions of life, which can only be found between the covers of the Bible.

The next two steps of Paul's command of applying God's Word to inspire others, rebuking and correcting, are the error-correcting processes. As students attempt to acquire truth, they will sometimes retain wrong or faulty information. At that point, we must rebuke and correct the error. We engage in this practice frequently, traditionally with red ink. Grading an assignment and determining what needs to be retaught is an important component of these two steps.

The principle behind this classroom practice is that we teach students a concept or skill and then provide opportunities for them to practice and demonstrate what they learned. The degree to which students display their understanding of a concept or application of a skill determines the percentage of mastery.

A standard must be established that measures student academic success. Ultimately, these standards of measurement are fixed. Either a student is able to calculate a sum or they do not. The student either knows the correct missing piece of information from a prompt or not. Even in the areas that allow opinions, personal interpretations, or theorization do not usurp the laws that God has written upon nature and in His Word.

The Bible is the ultimate standard. The doctrines (truthful teachings) found within Scripture are immutable, never to be altered by any person or force. People can resist believing in these truths, but that does not make them any less truthful. For example, someone might say, "God doesn't exist." This is an opinion the person can derive out of their volition, but it does not detract from the truth, or doctrine, of God's existence.

Correction and rebuke are important components in conforming to the Word of God. This can be the most unpleasant of the teaching process. The main reason is that it requires confrontation. Most people are uncomfortable with being corrected to any degree. Still, more dislike confrontation. However, teachers must bravely proclaim the truth of the Master Teacher and correct any derivation from it.

The final step is the culmination of Paul's response to biblical inspiration: training in righteousness. As our students are learning truth and are having their understanding of doctrines challenged or corrected, simultaneously, they must learn how to apply them to their lives.

Learning the truth of the Bible is an act of the mind and the heart. Far too many people have learned the principles of Scripture but never apply them to their lives. When this happens, no beneficial change occurs within that individual. It is like knowing the treatment needed to survive a horrible disease but refusing to submit to it to be cured. Accepting something to be true and applying that truth to your life can be two very different actions. The first step is mental assent, and the second is action.

Our students must be called to action. They must be equipped, trained, and inspired to delve deeper into the truth of God and thereby have their hearts and minds renewed. Like deft generals, we teachers rally those under our command and inspire them to pursue righteousness. To do that, we must also be trained in righteousness and study the Bible. God's Word is sufficient for the needs of both teachers and their students.

Empowering the Learner

During my career, it has been my honor to work with a wide range of learners. I have served students with severe and profound disabilities, others who were in gifted and talented programs, and still others who were in both groups. This maxim proved true time after time: *anyone can learn.*

However, danger can arise in the mind of the teacher who, intentionally or not, places his or her students into one of three groups: those who can learn, those who cannot learn, and those who will not learn. This mental classification on the part of the teacher is not a problem in itself. For example, a teacher must determine which students can perform a skill, those who cannot, and those who simply refuse. However, the danger creeps in when teachers form a binary conviction that some kids simply cannot learn.

No one would admit to such a belief, but it begins to reveal itself in the unguarded comments a teacher makes about a student:

"Jack simply can't divide." "Joann cannot tie her shoe." "They just don't get it." I often hear, "The poor baby just can't do it." Often, these are not statements about current academic progress but condemnations of a student's ability. Thankfully, these remarks are limited to a minority of teachers, but they serve to warn us of a negative outlook into which we can all fall.

Students will always respond to the expectations of their teachers. Either they will work hard to reach the goals a teacher sets for them, or they will fall into apathy and complacency. Studies show that effective teachers are the most important factor in student academic success.[42]

An effective teacher is someone who has a strong instructional skill set; good classroom management, a firm grasp on the content, the ability to assess student performance, and the ability to make necessary course corrections. As important as these characteristics are, they will never reach their fullest potency unless the teacher first empowers their students through inspiration. When students are inspired, they are empowered.

Chapter 8 discussion questions are the following:
1. What or whom inspired you to become an educator?
2. How have you inspired your students?
3. What success and challenges have you faced while trying to inspire your students?
4. What does "empowering the learner" mean to you?

CHAPTER 9

PASSION

I have often wondered what Jesus was like when He was not teaching the crowds or healing the sick. How did He recuperate after ministering with such grit, power, and energy? He taught with such passion and dedication; it must have been physically draining. Of all the characteristics of the Master Teacher, His passion amazes me the most as an educator.

Jesus was God in a body. He was fully human while fully possessing all the divine wisdom, virtue, and character of God. However, the gospels make it very clear that because He had a human body, He also had basic human needs. He knew what it was like to be hungry and thirsty. He felt strong emotions, and He grew tired. Did He ever experience discouragement? Did He ever lack drive or lose His passion to teach?

Throughout my career as an educator, I have often pondered these questions. Like every teacher, I have experienced exhaustion. I have suffered from frustration and lack of motivation. I have also fought overwhelming bouts of discouragement and even despair. In short, I have experienced the absence of passion.

Whenever I have tried to identify the reason for these hopeless feelings, I determined several causes: being frustrated with my students, their parents, the school, the lack of discipline, or even with other teachers. At various times, these can be contributing factors, but they are not the root cause. Usually at the center of my despair is the loss of passion.

Ignited Passion

If you ask a teacher why he or she decided to pursue a career in education, the overwhelming response is that they have a deep desire to learn and help others do likewise. Educators are passionate. No other vocation has a higher number of dedicated professionals who are interested in investing in other people.

Ask any teacher when they knew they wanted to be a teacher, and you will find that many knew from a young age they wanted to be an educator. Survey this same group and it becomes evident that each person can look back to a particular teacher who had inspired them to follow his or her example. Teachers impart passion to future teachers.

This process has endured from the beginning of human history. This ignited passion burns in the heart of a large number of teachers today. Even for those educators who cannot recall an early desire to teach, many of them can still point to a moment in which someone or something ignited their passion.

Teachers hold a torch lit by a past educator, and in turn, they ignite the torches of their students who will carry the passion to learn into the future. Passing the torch from one educator to another is proof to the living nature of education.

G. K. Chesterton illuminated the importance of this process: "Education is simply the soul of a society as it passes from one generation to another."[43] Teachers are responsible for preserving society's soul by infusing in their students the passion to learn and to teach.

Lost Passion

Despite this deep passion that many educators possess, going into their careers, an overwhelming number face burnout within the first few years. Long hours, limited resources, troublesome students, difficult parents, and lower wages are only a few factors contributing to many educators' decision to leave their profession prematurely.

No matter the factors that may have contributed to a teacher's decision to walk away, the ultimate reason is almost always the same: the passion they once had is dead. Let us face it: teaching is hard even when we are at the top of our game, but it is incredibly difficult, almost impossible, if we have lost our passion to teach.

As we have already explored, at its core, teaching is more than simply relaying facts and knowledge to students. It is the giving of hope, encouragement, and, most important, truth. Teachers do not simply assure the transfer of information from one thinking person to another; they impart passion.

Once a teacher has lost his or her passion to engage in this process, they are unable to fulfill their fundamental role as an educator. Sure, many teachers may for years go through the motions of informing their students, but they lack drive or passion. All of us know teachers who have been teaching for decades while their passion erodes day by day. They get to the point where they are simply doing their time until they can retire.

Over time, wind can steadily deplete the nutrient-rich topsoil resulting in infertile soil and poor crops. Similarly, the trials and frustrations of teaching slowly erode the teacher's passion. At the start of their careers, teachers possess a full measure of passion. Some teachers lose their passion after only a short time since their passion was superficial, like sand on a hillside. But even those teachers whose passion runs deep experience erosion along the way. Whether your loss of passion has been as quick as a mudslide or as slow and steady as the abrading of granite, I have great news! Your passion can be renewed.

As we look to Jesus, the Master Teacher, we see that He never lost His passion to teach. He was always available to those who came to Him for encouragement, hope, and instruction. He was never off His A-game. The force and passion of His didactic endeavors were just as strong at the beginning of His ministry as it was moments before His death on the cross. In short, His passion to serve others through His teaching never faded, never eroded.

How is this encouraging for us? Jesus offers us His grace in our role as teachers, the same grace He had as the Master Teacher. This does not mean we will never fail or experience apathy. On the contrary, experiencing dryness is to be expected occasionally. Yet just as an eroded hillside can be filled and restored, God's grace will fill us with the passion to teach His truth.

Here, it is important to clarify a detail. When we experience passionless exhaustion, we Christian teachers should never regard God's grace as a fast fix or a use-only-in-case-of-emergency solution. This perceives the grace of God as only a lifeboat to use once our own strength is used up. We must rely upon God's grace as a child relies on His mother or as all life on earth depends on the sun. God's grace alone is the source that empowers us to passionately serve Him as we teach others His truth.

Neither should we ignore the benefits of seeking rest and refreshment to renew our energies. Even Jesus sought times of rest and relaxation. He allowed Himself to have downtime and to get away from the pressures of teaching. He withdrew in order to press once again into the grace of His heavenly Father.

Fueling Passion

To answer the question I posed earlier in this chapter—"Did Jesus ever lose His passion to teach?"—the answer is a resounding no. Jesus did not lose His passion. He was the perfection of passion in human form. Although He was tempted to be discouraged—the Bible tells us that He was tempted in all things—He did not fall into that pit.

The word *passion* as it is now used first came from the Master Teacher's example. *Passion* is derived from a Latin root meaning "enduring sufferings." The word was first used to describe the sufferings of Christ during His crucifixion. Over the centuries, it shifted to denote intense enthusiasm or dedication. Jesus displayed such passion and dedication in His ministry that after he authenticated His words through His death and resurrection; the word *passion* encapsulated the example of Christ. His devotion to His ministry and act of redemption was so fierce that it became synonymous with *passion*.

That Jesus did not experience discouragement is wonderful news for His followers. What state would we be in if the source of all our hope experienced depression and discouragement? How could we reignite our passion if the Master Teacher was not able to maintain His passion? Thankfully, Jesus did not lose His passion, so we do not have to consider these questions.

God constantly empowered the passion Jesus demonstrated throughout His teaching ministry. There was never a time when the Master Teacher considered Himself removed from the grace of His Father. Likewise, we must daily, even moment by moment, ask for the grace of God in our lives so we might honor Him in our role as teachers. Especially during times when our passion is at its zenith, let's unceasingly seek God's grace.

Let's pause and consider what exactly God's grace is and why we should ask for it. In short, God's grace is His empowerment in the life of His followers to act in accordance with His will. As we have discussed in chapter 3, God is not only the giver of all truths, He is also the One who both desires and enables us to learn about all He has created, even about His nature. His grace is the driving force in this process. By it and through it, He takes flawed and sinful humans, who have no capability to act godly on their own, and empowers them to understand and walk in His ways.

This might sound like a lofty, perhaps even bizarre, comparison between the role of God's grace revealing His perfect nature to imperfect mortals and an elementary school teacher imparting mathematical facts to young children. However, in the giving of all truth, be it spiritual truths or empirical facts, God is involved. By God's grace, we are shown that He is the Holy One who created all there is, and by His grace, we learn that one plus one equals two.

If we ask for God's grace in our endeavors as teachers, will we never experience a loss of passion? No. Even though we are teachers, we are also students of seeking God's grace and applying it not only to our lives but also to our interactions with our students. We are imperfect and will experience passionless seasons of life. However, we have the promise that God is always with us and will refresh us with His grace.

As we have discovered, passion is an important factor in teaching. It is even contagious as it flows from us to our students. But we must never forget that passion is a byproduct of the grace of God. In ourselves, we do not possess an inexhaustible measure of passion. However, as Christian teachers, we know of passion's true source, and we have the promise of an unlimited supply of grace from God.

Chapter 9 discussion questions are the following:
1. Describe your passion.
2. What depletes you of your passion?
3. What has helped you reignite your passion for teaching?
4. How have you experienced God's grace as an educator?

CHAPTER *10*

HUMOR

Every seasoned teacher knows that a keen sense of humor is a key ingredient in working with students. Amid our frustrations, finding humor in our situation is often the best way of dealing with challenges. This was true for the Master Teacher who often faced frustrating situations that required a sense of humor.

One conspicuous example is found in the eighth chapter of the gospel of Mark. After teaching a large crowd of about four thousand people, Jesus miraculously fed the mass with seven loaves of bread and a few fish. After an encounter with a gaggle of Pharisees, He boarded a boat with His disciples. With the recent miracle and confrontation with the Pharisees still fresh in their minds, Jesus warned His disciples, "Watch out for the yeast of the Pharisees" (Mark 8:15 NIV). Jesus's reference to yeast was lost on His disciples. Mark tells us that the disciples discussed what Jesus could have meant by this warning. The best notion the disciples could come up with was to assume that Jesus mentioned yeast because they did not bring bread with them (see Mark 8:16). Any teacher can understand the frustration of the disciples' remarks. They missed the point. There was a disparity between what the Master Teacher communicated and what the disciples understood. This reveals the importance of using humor in education as it greases the wheels of the entire learning process for both the teacher and the student.

What Is Humor?

How would you define humor? It seems like that should be an easy task, doesn't it? After all, it is a phenomenon that everyone experiences and virtually everyone enjoys. Many actively seek it, evidenced by the numerous social media posts that prompt us to respond with a laughing emoji. Others investigate humor as a serious academic topic. Great philosophers like Plato, Aristotle, and Kant have all tried to define humor and determine its origin.

My inquiry into the topic of humor in education was in no way a search for philosophical understanding of humor. I became interested in it the more I relished the humor I experienced as a teacher and how prevalent it was in the gospel accounts of Jesus's teaching. When I first began to ponder how to define humor and its role within my classroom, the best I could concoct were synonyms such as "funny," "amusement," "playfulness," "enjoyment," and even "joking." Laced through all these was an elemental concept of humor, but they seemed to be only the results of humor and failed to describe its true impetus.

In his insightful work, *The Screwtape Letters*, C. S. Lewis states, "Humour involves a sense of proportion and a power of seeing yourself from the outside."[44] When I first read this, a light bulb flashed above my head. Lewis (my favorite author) reveals an undeniable truth about humor: it is the juxtaposition of what is normal or consistent with what is different or amplified.

A joke is humorous because the punch line is an exaggeration or inconsistency from the setup and premise. We find humor in our situations because they differ in degree to those we usually encounter. Comedians make their living from making observations from human experiences and inviting others to see these experiences from an excessive angle. Observational comedy and the whole "what's the deal with x" routine capitalizes on this function of humor by inviting people to see their lives from a different or overblown perspective.

Thanks to Lewis's explanation of humor, we can construe how humor arises in our classrooms and how we might use it to benefit our students and ourselves. We can appreciate humorous disproportions because nowhere are they more abundant than in education.

Finding Humor in Education

Humor permeates a teacher's experience due to the core nature of our job. As we discussed in chapter 3, we are in the business of proclaiming truth and equipping our students with the skills to find it in the world around them. As our students learn truth, they emerge from ignorance to apply their skills.

As our students progress through this process, the pitfalls of misunderstanding and unfamiliarity can produce amusing comparisons. The example at the beginning of this chapter proves this point. The disciples were underway in this learning process but frequently displayed sharp misunderstanding. It is obvious to the reader that Jesus taught using recent experiences. His disciples were not prepared to listen and could offer only a naïve response.

Before we come down too hard on the disciples, we should appreciate this same amusing proportion in ourselves. Think back when you were in school. Reflect upon things you once regarded as true and compare them to what you later discovered to be correct. I remember when I discovered in a second-grade science unit that dogs were not all boys and cats were not all girls. I had firmly believed this presumption and was amused at how wrong I had been. The rest of my school days held similar revelations that were just as amusing. When I reflect on my former misunderstandings against what I now know, I find joy in that retrospection. I do not look back on my misunderstandings or those of my students to ridicule the ignorance. On the contrary, enjoyment is found in witnessing the evolution of the learner.

The humor we embrace within our classrooms should never be the type that disparages students. Rather, it should be the byproduct of a deep understanding and respect a teacher has for his or her students and to be used as a means to encourage them. Keeping the whole process of students' learning in view, good teachers will recognize the beginning state of the students, their current rate of learning, and the ultimate goals they should obtain. Finding humor in this process is simply enjoying the phases of comprehension and mastery through which the student progresses.

Additionally, humor is a powerful tool for the students themselves. Let us return to Lewis's definition: "Humour involves a sense of proportion *and a power of seeing yourself from the outside*" (emphasis mine). We have seen how everyone involved in the learning process must understand humor as a quality of proportion. The next part of the definition concerns the individual learner.

The students must have the self-awareness to enjoy the quality of humor present in their own learning. Again, this awareness must build its foundation upon proportion. Students benefit when they understand where they are in the process of learning in comparison with what they are aiming for. This is the power of seeing oneself from the outside.

Another benefit of a student's self-awareness is the ownership they adopt in their own learning. This is a natural result from knowing where you are and where you need to be. In essence, students with this self-awareness have a map marked with a big dot that says, "You are here" and an X on where they are to end up. The way between the two points is unknown or obscure to them. It is the job of their teachers to equip them for their journey and help them navigate their way. The journey is fraught with joy and humor to those who know to look for both.

As teachers, we must awaken our students' perception of this joy and humor. This, like many fundamental concepts, is a process that is caught more than it is taught. Every student has a sense of humor. Some have it to such a degree that it is their most distinguishing characteristic. In other students, it is barely detectable. Yet inasmuch as every student can learn, every student can discover joy and humor in their learning.

How do we awaken and foster humorous joy within our classrooms? First, know that we use humor all the time even when we do not realize it. Whenever we are trying to explain a difficult concept or present an abstract idea, we often reach for an analogy to aid our students' understanding. This is teaching in proportion.

By appealing to what the students know, we can lead them on the journey to where they need to be. In my experience of both teaching and observing teachers in the classroom, these comparisons are often so exaggerated that they are comical. Seemingly, the greater (funnier) the exaggeration, the better the students can make the connection and comprehend. Even if these comparisons do not always entice our students to laugh out loud, the pleasant subtle humor found within the presentation assures that they remember the content.

How Jesus Used Humor

With an understanding of humor and its role in education, let us continue to focus on how the Master Teacher used His amazing sense of humor. It might sound odd to make this claim, especially to those who picture Him as a stoic proclaimer of truth, but there again is the principle of humor, by proportion, exhibited. If asked to describe the Lord's teaching style, many of us would picture Him as a sullen, aloof figure who taught in a dull, even voice. Thanks to cinematic depictions and classical art, we might envision Him as a gaunt and pale character who never smiled and probably spoke with a British accent. This is very different from the strong, bold, and humorous carpenter who was the Son of God. The Master Teacher laughed, smiled, and enjoyed teaching.

If one method of teaching could summarize Jesus's style, it would be the use of parables. He constantly told stories of people in situations His hearers would understand, sometimes acting in ways that made sense to them while other times doing something that was considered shocking or taboo, all to prove a deeper truth. Clearly, He desired His students to hear the stories and compare these truths on their own. Through the engagement of comparing the plots of the parables to the underlying truth they revealed, the learners were actively involved in not only hearing the truth but applying it to their minds and lives. Although there is no overt, laugh-out-loud forms humor displayed in most of these parables, the rule of proportionality in humor was always at play.

The Master Teacher used humor in His didactic presentations. The Gospel of Matthew is rich with humorous examples. Jesus underscored blatant hypocrisy by describing a man who tries to remove a small speck of sawdust out of his friend's eye while the whole time has a large plank protruding out of his own eye (Matthew 7:5). Presenting the picture of a camel going through the eye of a needle (19:24), Jesus showcased the inability of someone to honor God when the person loves money more than God. A more positive example of how Jesus used humor was in declaring to His disciples that if they had faith the size of a mustard seed, they could command the mountains to be moved (17:20).

The humor used in the proportion of one thing to one another is perfect. Consider the comparisons: the speck of dust that floats in the air versus a large plank of wood, the huge beast of burden and a tiny feature of one of the smallest of household utensils, and one of the smallest seeds with huge vistas filling the horizon. Such vast proportions between these paired items engage the learner's sense of humor while underscoring deeper truths.

If the Master Teacher used humor to teach the deepest truth ever presented to humanity, how can we do less?

Chapter 10 discussion questions are the following:
1. What humorous examples have you experienced within the classroom?
2. How do you use humor when you are teaching?
3. What are your experiences of your students finding joy as they learn?

CHAPTER *11*

FEARLESSNESS

The gospels record numerous occasions when religious and educational leaders confronted Jesus. The tension within these accounts is palpable. These men foolishly accused the Master Teacher of committing a number of sins from violating the Jewish law to associating with societal outcasts (see Matthew 9:10–11, 11:19) which only showed their blindness to the Word of God and revealed their desire to stop Jesus from teaching. They circled the Master Teacher like ravenous wolves, waiting and watching for anything they could use to strike.

Jesus did not shy away from them. Whenever the attacks came, He defended Himself with masterful responses that left His accusers speechless, even embarrassed, because their hypocrisy and true intent became evident. Some attacks were absurd. The Pharisees condemned Jesus for healing a sick person on the Sabbath (see Mark 3:1–6).

Jesus was not always just on the defensive. Oftentimes, He boldly reacted to those who willfully disobeyed God's commands. A colorful example of His being on the offense is His clearing the temple of moneychangers who monetized the worship of God (see John 2:13–22). The sound of coins clinking as they exchanged hands and the voices of men bartering were silenced with an eruption of fury. Those involved in the perversion of worship scattered as the young rabbi flipped tables and dispersed livestock. With a whip of cords gripped in His strong hand, He fearlessly drove out all those who turned a place of worship into a marketplace.

In His boldness and resolution to proclaim truth and defy all who opposed God's Word, not once did the Master Teacher back down or turn tail. Jesus possessed godly grit because He is Truth.

Please note that even in His strong, fearless confrontations, Jesus always acted wisely. He never responded blindly or irrationally. His reactions were calculated and proportional to His divine character. He was fearless because God the Father was with Him as He proclaimed the truth.

Godly fearlessness embraces wisdom. It clings to the truth of God and does not remain quiet on unpopular issues. Fearlessness tips the scales permanently toward caring what God says over what humans say or do. Our Lord was truly fearless because He lacked the fear of what others would do to Him or say about Him.

Fearlessness, as the Master Teacher displayed it, is boldness and resolution in declaring the truth of God to the abandonment of concern of what others might say or do.

Facing Fear

It is interesting to consider the various fears and phobias from which people suffer. Some are common to everyone: fear of loss, fear of death, or fear of real or perceived danger. Others are more specific to the individual and relate to personal preference: fear of flying or fear of snakes or some other creepy-crawly. All fears, common and specific, share a universal root: whatever is feared will harm us.

Some of our fears are legitimate. We have either been harmed or could realistically be harmed by the object of our fear. These are what we call rational fears; for example, the fear of losing your job or the fear of having no money. Irrational fears, however, have a low probability of happening. These are fears like having an elevator cable snap while on it or allowing a fear of needles to keep you from a doctor's appointment. For all of us, it is a mixed bag. We suffer from both rational and irrational fears.

If we are to be fearless as Jesus was, are we to simply ignore our fears, pretend they don't exist? Not at all. We can be aware of our fears, but we must relegate them to their proper place.

The Master Teacher taught that we should not fear those who could harm or kill the body; rather, we should fear God, the righteous Judge (see Luke 12:4–5). This is the dividing line. Unchecked fears have the power to control us body, soul, and mind. When we fear someone or something other than God, we allow that fear to control us. We listen to it instead of rightly respecting God. Who would you rather fear: someone or something that has no eternal power over you or a holy, loving God who desires your eternal good?

Many people, even Christians, believe that fearing God is an outdated or foolish belief. They maintain that if God is good, He should not be feared. This is an error because it contradicts Jesus's command:

> I tell you, my friends, do not fear those who kill the body, and after that have nothing more that they can do. But I will warn you whom to fear: fear Him who, after He has killed, has authority to cast into hell. Yes, I tell you, fear Him!" (Luke 12:4–5)

When Jesus instructed us to "fear" God and not to "fear" anyone or anything else, He used the same word: *phobeō*. Does this Greek word look familiar? We derive "phobia" from it. Fear is fear. It is not a sin to fear, but it is a sin to fear the wrong thing.

To fear God is to understand that He is a holy Judge who rightly condemns sinful humanity, including you and me. It is only by His grace that we have been saved from this judgment. Understanding this relationship reveals both the depth of God's love and why it is proper to respect, or fear, Him.

Martin Luther distinguished between two kinds of fear people often experience in connection with God: the *servile* fear and *filial* fear.[45] Servile fear is the terror of a prisoner under hard punishment. It is the anxiety of the condemned in the presence of his tormentor.

Whether or not the punishment is justified is not the issue. The issue is fear. This is the fear that many people experience when considering that God judges all sin. Theologian and teacher R. C. Sproul describes the role this type of fear has to a nonbeliever:

> We fear God because he is holy. Our fear is not the healthy fear the Bible encourages us to have. Our fear is a servile fear—a fear born of dread. God is too great for us; he is too awesome… In his presence we quake and tremble. Meeting him personally may be our greatest trauma.[46]

Filial fear is based on family dynamics (hence the name, which is derived from the Latin word pertaining to sons and daughters). It is the reverence and respect of a son or daughter toward their loving father. This is the fear a Christian has to God, whom they call "Father." The Apostle Paul reminded the Roman Christians that they "did not receive a spirit of slavery to fall back into fear, but you have received the Spirit of adoptions of sons, by whom we cry, 'Abba! Father!'" (Romans 8:15).

As Christians, the love and respect we have for our heavenly Father begins with servile fear: we know we deserve punishment for our sins. But because of God's loving-kindness and glory, He put our punishment on Jesus so He could redeem us and adopt us into His family. At this point, our fear changes. We no longer fear what is not of God, but we honor and respect the holy God.

As Christian teachers, we honor our Lord best when we acknowledge, confess, and turn away from the fears that take our focus off Him and His holiness. As followers and emulators of the Master Teacher, we can proclaim truth with certainty, boldness, and confidence because of His sacrifice on our behalf.

Confidence

Crippling fear that prevents us from speaking the truth is not what God desires from His followers. The Apostle Paul reminded his student in the faith, Timothy, who likewise taught others, "For God has not given us a spirit of fear, but one of power, love, and sound judgment" (2 Timothy 1:7). Paul's admonishment serves to remind us of the confidence we have in Christ.

When we fear God and have proper respect for Him, we are freed from the idolatry of fearing anything or anyone else. The spirit of fear that Paul warned Timothy against is replaced by the Holy Spirit. As God's Spirit dwells within us and instills in us a sound mind, we experience His love and power. A sound mind gives us the confidence to boldly transmit truth.

Since true confidence comes from a correct fear (respect) of God, we can have assurance without arrogance. Having confidence is not prideful if we recognize its source. We will not know all the answers to all the questions and challenges we will encounter, but we have full assurance, confidence, and trust in the One who does.

When our confidence is established upon God's grace, and not our own ability, we can rest in the guarantee that we may proclaim truth without faltering. This is essential for teachers. As the purveyors and communicators of truth to our students, we must teach effectively and confidently. If we are unsure of our ability to teach truth, we are ineffective.

Confrontations

We have all experienced the sickening sensation. It comes the moment we must affirm an unpopular truth or perspective at the expense of being accepted by others. Almost everyone faces this struggle first within the school setting, and the sensation never fully leaves us. It is the feeling we experience when confronting error by telling the truth.

It only stands to reasons that Christians will encounter this more than anyone else since truth is seldom popular. As we have discussed in chapter 3, there is an ongoing attack on truth. Proclaiming truth requires denying falsehoods. It requires affirming all that is aligned with the Word of God and decrying all that opposes His Word. To announce what is right necessitates illuminating what is wrong. Confrontations are inevitable.

Some seem to confront falsehood with ease and diplomacy. Yet most of us shy away from confrontations even when we know we are completely in the right. It is not that we do not want the truth to be told or that we do not think it worth our time. We become afraid of what others might think about us. This need to be approved by others is deeply ingrained in all of us. It is rooted in the longing to be loved and accepted. This longing is not wrong in and of itself; however, when this longing replaces our duty to proclaim truth, that is when we have slipped into sin.

We live in a fallen world. We will not be accepted or loved by everyone, especially if we espouse unpopular truths. This is when we must consider the balance. Is it more important to be accepted by the vast majority or to fearlessly proclaim truth? Should we remain silent and not confront others with the truth, or should we be willing to confront them with it?

I am not advocating militancy. Far from it. As Christian teachers, we should not pick fights. However, when the fight comes to us, we are to fearlessly confront error and those espousing it. To prepare us for the inevitable confrontations, the Master Teacher promised that we will not be alone.

When they bring you before the synagogues and the rulers and the authorities, do not worry about how or what you are to speak in your defense, or what you are to say; for the Holy Spirit will teach you in that very hour what you ought to say. (Luke 12:11 NASB)

> We can be fearless when we face confrontations as we defend truth because the Holy Spirit promises to be with us.

Chapter 11 discussion questions are the following:

1. When have you witnessed fearlessness in an educator? What did he or she do and say?
2. What kind(s) of fear hinders you from proclaiming truth?
3. How do you exercise confidence when you teach?
4. What keeps you from being confident?
5. How do you confront people when necessary?
6. How have you defended the truth?

CHAPTER *12*

GO...AND TEACH

Wonder, excitement, and a renewed sense of purpose and passion must have seized the disciples as they listened to their resurrected Master Teacher. All that He had taught them and every miracle they had witnessed washed over the disciples as Jesus spoke, driving home that His teachings were more than mere words, more than aphorisms or good moral stories. His claims were not idle boasts but the promises of the loving holy God to His servants. He was not a ghost or some other phantasm but flesh and blood. And His flesh bore the scars from the wounds they had seen Him receive just weeks before.

Jesus Christ, the Master Teacher, raised from the dead, stood before His disciples, proving that all He had taught was true. Through His death, burial, and resurrection, He authenticated His claim to be the Truth. Likewise, all that He had instructed was similarly confirmed. The resurrection of Christ verified His role as the Master Teacher.

The earthly ministry of the Master Teacher was complete. He fulfilled the mission of His heavenly Father. Before He was taken into heaven, Jesus gave His students a final command:

> All power is given to me in heaven and upon earth. *Go ye therefore and teach* all nations, baptizing them in the name of the Father, and of the Son, and of the Holy Spirit. *Teaching* them to

observe all things whatever I have commanded you: and lo, I am with you always, *even* to the end of the world. Amen. (Matthew 28:18–20 KJV, emphasis mine)

Now it was the disciples' turn. They had spent three years with Jesus in preparation for the next stage of His mission. He was sending His disciples out as teachers. Jesus Christ, the Teacher of teachers, appointed His followers to follow His example and to teach the truth of the gospel.

This is the beginning chapter of Christian teachers. This is the dawn of the task we, as teachers who are followers of Christ, are honored to keep. The Great Commission Jesus gave His disciples to go out and teach others did not stop with the men gathered on that mountainside. It echoes throughout history and continues to this day. It has been passed down to us by generations of teachers who have faithfully followed the Master Teacher's example. The ultimate goal of this movement is the establishment of Christ's kingdom.

A Kingdom Education

The establishment of the kingdom of God was at the center of all Jesus taught. Throughout His ministry, the virtue He taught, the parables He told, even the miracles He performed all pointed to a coming kingdom He would establish. Professor Daniel Wallace puts the Master Teacher's desire into perspective:

> Jesus did teach about values…but he also put them in a context. These were not abstract principles; rather, they penetrated like a surgeon's scalpel into the heart and soul of the person. Nothing illustrates this more than Jesus' teaching about the kingdom of God, which all scholars agree was the most basic theme of his teaching.[47]

If this theme was so important to our Lord, how can it be any less to us?

As Christian teachers, we are kingdom teachers. In all of our striving to educate others, we bear the divine command to teach others the truth of Christ and to guide them into His kingdom.

What exactly is the kingdom to which our Master Teacher was referring? It is His kingdom. His kingdom is a present reality that will one day become the only government. Right now, Christ reigns in the hearts of all Christians. He gave His followers the task to teach others about His kingdom and invite them to allow Christ to reign in their hearts. One day, He will establish an actual governmental system from which He will reign. Until that day, His followers await the return of their King. We are citizens of Christ's kingdom and ambassadors who have been tasked to represent Him until He returns.

The royal decree is proclaimed. The King has designated every Christian to be His disciple and to spread His kingdom by teaching others. Therefore, every Christian is a teacher. Those of us who are formal educators are expected to follow His example all the more.

As we teach, even the most elemental and mundane of lessons, we must maintain this kingdom perspective focused in our minds. As we teach truth, remember that we are explaining a character of God that is exemplified in His kingdom. When we strive to be better communicators, we are honing in our skills as diplomats and ambassadors for God's purposes. When we form relationships with others, we are to inspire and love them as Christ loves us thus representing the hallmark of His kingdom.

Go...

It is a simple command. The Master Teacher did not leave any room for misunderstanding or exclusion. To everyone who follows Him, He has given a succinct and undeniable mandate: "Go." The command is not "if you are going" or even "when you are going," it is an intentional and active order to go. The Greek command is best translated "after you have gone."[48] Clearly, Jesus intended His followers to be active and purposeful in teaching and making disciples. His command left no room for passivity. As the great missionary Hudson Taylor is attributed as saying, "The Great Commission is not an option to be considered; it is a command to be obeyed."

Every time we walk into our classrooms, our Lord's command should ring in our ears.

"Go!"

When we prepare to teach our lessons or present our lectures, it reverberates.

"Go!"

Especially when we wrestle with the challenges while we have the honor to proclaim truth, the Master Teacher's command resonates in every fiber of our being.

"Go!"

This mandate might require us to travel from our homes or to remain in the same town our whole lives. Some Christians answer this call through international missions and others by simply walking next door. Our directive to go means we are active participants in expanding Christ's kingdom—from the vast metropolis to the single home.

The Lord intends His followers to teach in every nation. His directive is global. As we advance His kingdom, let's be cautious and remember that we are moving into enemy-occupied territory. An enemy who opposes the growth of God's kingdom will try to counter any move we make. However, the army of the Master Teacher is assured victory. From the exploratory forces of missionaries to the Christians who live in those lands, the kingdom of God is growing.

Wherever we are placed and in whatever situation we are in, we are told to be active in instructing others in the Gospel of the Master Teacher. In Christ's estimation, there are no retired teachers; none are decommissioned. We are always teachers.

When we obey this command to go, we discover a grand adventure. One that might not always be easy, and at times, we might be tempted to despair, but the Master Teacher has promised to be with us.

...and Teach

Am I elevating our task as educators to an unrealistic degree? Am I making the role of a teacher something it is not? I think not. Anything humans aim to do to exalt Christ and make Him known is the most important activity we can undertake.

When educators see their role for what God intends it to be, the nobility of our profession is recovered. Teaching was designed to be an act of worship because, in its true form, it proclaims the truth and character of God.

My fellow educators, we have the honor of worshiping the Master Teacher by following His example. We have the joy of partaking in the act of imparting both knowledge and wisdom to those whom God has entrusted to us. Nothing is more beautiful or fulfilling than knowing the Master Teacher more and more and serving as He served.

Go!

Go discover and worship Jesus the Master Teacher.

Go communicate His truth.

Go and lead with love, compassion, and humor.

Go with a fearless passion that inspires others.

Go...and teach!

Chapter 12 discussion questions are the following:
1. How are you obeying the Master Teacher's command to "go...and teach?"
2. How are you continuing the heritage of Christian teachers?
3. With Christ's kingdom in view, how are you preparing for His coming kingdom?
4. What do you need to do, what preparations do you need to make to go and teach?

NOTES

Chapter 2

1. Frederick Pollock, *Spinoza: His Life and Philosophy* (London: C. Kegan Paul & Co. 1880), 366.
2. Ignatius to the Ephesians 15.1
3. Clement of Alexandria, "The Instructor," Chapter XII
4. Martin Luther, *A Commentary on St. Paul's Epistle to the Galatians* (Grand Rapids, MI: Christian Classics Ethereal Library), 16.
5. John Calvin, *The Institutes of the Christian Religion* (Grand Rapids, MI: Christian Classics Ethereal Library), 174.
6. E. L. Kemp, *History of Education* (Philadelphia: J. B. Lippincott, 1901), 101.
7. Roy B. Zuck, *Teaching as Jesus Taught* (Eugene, Oregon: Wipf and Stock Publishers, 2002).
8. What Do Americans Believe About Jesus? 5 Popular Beliefs https://www.barna.com/research/what-do-americans-believe-about-jesus-5-popular-beliefs/
9. C. S. Lewis, *Mere Christianity* (New York, NY: Harper Collins Publishers, 2000).
10. Thomas B. Warren, *Jesus: The Lamb Who Is a Lion* (Jonesboro, TN: National Christian Press, 1988), 114.
11. William Barclay, *Jesus as They Saw Him* (Grand Rapids, MI: Eerdmans Publishing, 1962).
12. Francis Brown, Samuel Driver, Charles Briggs, The Brown-Drivers-Briggs Hebrew and English Lexicon—page 912. H7231 (Grand Rapids, MI: Hendrickson Publishers, 1996), 912.
13. In fact, they were titles that were first used in the period of the Tannaim (AD 10–220). See Drazin, *History of Jewish Education* (Franklin Classics Trade, 1940) 36.
14. Ibid., 11–13.
15. Avot 1:4; from https://www.sefaria.org/Pirkei_Avot.1?lang=bi

[16] Christopher Day, *Developing Teachers: The Challenges of Lifelong Learning* (London: Falmer Press, 1999), 2.

Chapter 3

[17] John F. MacArthur, *The Truth War: Fighting for Certainty in an Age of Deception* (Nashville, TN: Thomas Nelson, 2007) 2.
[18] Francis A. Schaeffer, *How Should We Then Live?* (Wheaton, Il: Crossway Books, 2005), 132.
[19] James Strong, #3506, *Strong's Exhaustive Concordance of the Bible* (Grand Rapids: Zondervan, 2004). Joseph H. Thayer, "Logos," *Thayer's Greek-English Lexicon* (Grand Rapids: Baker Book Group, 1977).
[20] Mark Regnerus, "How different are the adult children of parents who have same-sex relationships?" Findings from the New Family Structures Study, https://doi.org/10.1016/j.ssresearch.2012.03.009.
[21] Will Durant, The Story of Philosophy (New York, NY: Pocket Books, 2006).

Chapter 4

[22] C. S. Lewis, *The Abolition of Man* (New York: Macmillan Publishing, 1978).
[23] Bill and Melinda Gates Foundation (2014). *Primary sources: America's teachers on teaching in an era of change: A project of Scholastic and the Bill and Melinda Gates Foundation* (3rd ed.), http://www.scholastic.com/primarysources/download-the-full-report.htm
[24] Guy Claxton, *Teaching to Learn: A Direction for Education* (Cassell Education Series), 27.
[25] Herman H. Horne, *Jesus, the Master Teacher* (Los Angeles: HardPress Publishing, 2012), 51.
[26] James Strong, #33846, "paraballō," *Strong's Exhaustive Concordance of the Bible* (Grand Rapids: Zondervan, 2004).

Chapter 5

[27] Albert Mohler, *The Conviction to Lead: 25 Principles for Leadership That Matters* (Minneapolis, MN: Bethany House Publishers, 2014).
[28] James Strong, #5273, "hypocrite," *Strong's Exhaustive Concordance of the Bible*. Joseph H. Thayer, "hypocrite," Thayer's Greek-English Lexicon.
[29] Aristotle, *The Nicomachean Ethics* (Cambridge, MA: Harvard University Press, 2003).

30 Plato, *The Republic* Book III (London: Penguin Classics, 2003), 100.
31 C. S. Lewis, *The Abolition of Man,* "Illustrations of the Tao," 95.

Chapter 6

32 Richard Sibbes, *The Returning Backslider* (Lafayette, IN: Sovereign Grace Publishers, 1967), 79.
33 George Thomas Kurian and Mark A. Lamport, "Love," *Encyclopedia of Christian Education* (Rowman & Littlefield: Lanham, 2015), 763.
34 The three gospels are Matthew, Mark, and Luke. These three are known as the Synoptic gospels due to the high degree of shared material. Matthew 9:36, 14:14, 15:32, 20:35; Mark 1:41, 6:34, 8:2, 9:22; Luke 7:13, 10:33, 15:20.
35 James Strong, #4697, "*splagchnizomai*," *Strong's Concordance.* Joseph H. Thayer, "*splagchnizomai*," *Thayer's Greek Lexicon.*
36 James C. Dobson, *New Dare to Discipline* (Wheaton, IL: Tyndale House Publishers, 2014), 6.
37 James Strong, #4637, *Strong's Concordance.* Joseph H. Thayer, "ditto," *Thayer's Greek Lexicon.*
38 Clayton R. Cook, Susanna Coco, Yanchen Zhang, Aria E. Fiat, Mylien T. Duong, Tyler L. Renshaw, Anna C. Long, and Sophia Frank, "Cultivating Positive Teacher–Student Relationships: Preliminary Evaluation of the Establish–Maintain–Restore (EMR) Method," *School Psychology Review:* September 2018, Vol. 47, No. 3, 226–43.
39 Brian A. Primack, Ariel Shensa, Jaime E. Sidani, Erin O. Whaite, Liu Yi Lin, Daniel Rosen, Jason B. Colditz, Ana Radovic, and Elizabeth Miller, "Social Media Use and Perceived Social Isolation Among Young Adults in the U.S," *American Journal of Preventive Medicine* 53, no. 1 (July 2017): 1–8. doi:10.1016/j.amepre.2017.01.010.

Chapter 7

40 Thomas H. Groome, *Christian Religious Education* (San Francisco, CA: Harper & Row, 1980), 115.

Chapter 8

41 *Oxford Latin Dictionary*, (1982), S.V. "*inspirare.*"
42 Find study

Chapter 9

[43] G. K. Chesterton, *The Illustrated London News* (London, 1924).

Chapter 10

[44] C. S. Lewis, *The Screwtape Letters* (New York: HarperOne, 2013).

Chapter 11

[45] Martin Luther, *Select Works on Martin Luther: An Offering to the Church of God in "The Last Days"* (London, 1826), 535.
[46] R. C. Sproul, *The Holiness of God* (Wheaton, IL: Tyndale House, 1998), 45.

Chapter 12

[47] Darrell L. Bock and Daniel B. Wallace, *Dethroning Jesus: Exposing Popular Cultures Quest to Unseat the Biblical Christ* (Nashville: Thomas Nelson, 2010), 132–33.
[48] The Greek word *poreuthentes* is an aorist participle. Daniel B. Wallace, "The Great Commission or the Great Suggestion?" https://danielbwallace.com/2014/02/17/the-great-commission-or-the-great-suggestion/.

ABOUT THE AUTHOR

Timothy Wade grew up in central Texas—the same region many members of his family have served as pastors and teachers for over 125 years. Timothy followed this heritage by becoming an educator and discovering the joys of serving and worshipping Jesus as a teacher.

He furthered this interest in both his role as a student with earned degrees in biblical studies, theology, and education and his vocation as a teacher, administrator, and educational consultant.

Timothy and his wife, Kara, live in Texas with their three children.

CPSIA information can be obtained
at www.ICGtesting.com
Printed in the USA
BVHW071455130423
662291BV00006B/402